THE ESSENCE *of* BUDDHA

THE PATH *to* ENLIGHTENMENT

RYUHO OKAWA

IRH Press

First U.S. edition with updates in 2016

Published under the same title in Great Britain in 2002 by Time Warner Books
Published by Time Warner Paperbacks in 2003

Originally published in Japan as *Shaka No Honshin* by IRH Press Co., Ltd., in August 1988 and republished under the same title in October 1997.

IRH PRESS
New York

Library of Congress Cataloging-in-Publication Data

ISBN 13: 978-1942125-06-8
ISBN 10: 1-942125-06-2

Printed in Turkey
First edition
Seventh printing

Cover Design: Whitney Cookman

Contents

THREE

THE SIX PARAMITAS

FOUR

THE CONCEPT *of* THE VOID

FIVE

THE LAW *of* CAUSALITY

SIX

THE PHILOSOPHY *of* HUMAN PERFECTION

Preface to the Current Edition

This book was written in simple language to offer modern people an accessible explanation of Shakyamuni Buddha's inner thoughts. The topics that are covered here include teachings from both the Theravada and Mahayana schools of Buddhism. Both of these philosophies have spread widely over the several hundred years since Shakyamuni's death, and both have had teachings added to them by later generations. But the essence of both schools originated in his own teachings during his life, as well as his own guidance from heaven to his disciples on Earth.

It is my hope that this book will offer you an introduction, with a unique flavor, to Buddhist philosophy. In closing, I would like to add my prediction that the arrogance and disrespect of the modern age will not last much longer.

Ryuho Okawa
Master and CEO of Happy Science Group
October 1997

Preface to the Original Edition

It gives me great joy to publish this book, *The Essence of Buddha*. I have used simple language to elucidate Shakyamuni's core teachings so that a newcomer to Buddhism will have little trouble grasping their essence. This book offers an overview of his entire philosophy and gives you a clear outline of his teachings. In the first chapter, I have told the story of Shakyamuni's ascetic life and inner journey to great enlightenment; then, in the following chapters, I have explained the essence of his teachings as a way of life for modern people. These teachings include the Eightfold Path, the Six Paramitas, the void, and the law of causality. In the future, I would also like to offer a more complete account of Shakyamuni's life.

I wrote this book based on what was spiritually revealed to me, as were *The Laws of the Sun*, *The Golden Laws*, and *The Nine Dimensions*. It is my deepest hope that many people who read this book will find nourishment for their hearts and minds from within the pages that follow.

Ryuho Okawa
Master and CEO of Happy Science Group
August 1988

THE JOURNEY *to* ENLIGHTENMENT

The Renunciation

In this book, I would like to explore the inner world of Gautama Siddhartha as I take you through his journey to enlightenment and his life thereafter. You may actually know him more commonly as the Buddha and he is also known as Shakyamuni Buddha. I will keep the details about Shakyamuni's history and life circumstances simple to give prominence to his inner world and allow us to delve into his true thoughts. What went through the mind of Shakyamuni when he embarked on the ascetic life, and how did he reach enlightenment? What was he thinking, and how did he live during the decades that followed his enlightenment—the period when he was preaching his teachings?

There are many books that describe how Shakyamuni renounced worldly life to become an ascetic seeker, and 80 percent of what is told in them is true. In this chapter, I would like to look further into the true reasons for his decision to become an ascetic. He made this decision for three reasons. The first reason came from an inner voice. His heart ached with anticipation for a higher purpose to his life—a calling he was born to fulfill. And he realized that the comforts and luxuries of royal life would keep him from fulfilling this higher purpose. He could not ignore the deep inner urge he felt to seek out this unknown future that awaited him. His experience may resemble the determined aspirations of an ambitious young man setting off from his rural hometown in pursuit of great achievement. And his decision also came from an inherent sense of knowing. He had a strong premonition that he was being called to accomplish something of great worth to the world.

What was his second reason? The scriptures about Shakyamuni Buddha's life describe his renunciation of worldly life with an allegory about how he discovered the four forms of human suffering—birth, aging, illness, and death—when he was twenty-nine: "There were four gates at the Kapilavastu palace. At the east gate, he met an enfeebled man suffering from old age. Then, at the south gate, he met the diseased and saw their suffering. At the west gate, he saw an ailing man facing death. And finally, at the north gate, he saw an ascetic." According to legend, these encounters made him wonder why suffering existed. At the age of twenty-nine, this was supposedly the first time he had ever seen these states of suffering. But if this were true, it would have been absurd that he had lived for so long before noticing the existence of suffering.

The real story was different. The palace of Kapilavastu, Shakyamuni's home, had a custom of inviting ascetics who were known for their enlightenment to speak and share their wisdom every month. It was similar to the Japanese imperial family's tradition of inviting people to give lectures. Shakyamuni joined the members of the royal family and listened to the talks of these ascetic teachers. But even though many people were deeply moved and impressed by what they taught, he couldn't help but keep thinking about his philosophical questions and wished he could find out more. What were these ascetics in search of? What was true enlightenment? He wasn't fully convinced by their teachings, and he longed to find the answers to his questions. This was the main reason he chose to become an ascetic.

The third reason was a strong desire for solitude that would allow him to reflect deeply within himself. Shakyamuni always had a meditative disposition; since his early teenage years, he had been fond of contemplating and liked to be by himself, absorbed in thought. However, since the royal customs of his time required the prince to take wives, formal wedding ceremonies had been held for him, and he had taken four wives. His first royal wife was Yashodhara, who was followed by Gopa, then Manodhara, and finally, a beautiful royal mistress, Murgaja, who had been an attendant.

During Shakyamuni's time, it was a custom for kings and princes to have several wives for four important reasons: 1) to increase the chances of securing a royal heir; 2) to protect the king and princes from enemy ambushes during the night by having several palaces in different locations, each with a wife; 3) to reduce each wife's influence on government decisions; and 4) to demonstrate the king's stateliness. The first wife Shakyamuni married was the beautiful Gopa. Then, he married the dignified Yashodhara, who came from an aristocratic family. He took her as his first lady, and she would later become a nun, following the path of her son Rahula, who became a monk. Rahula was Shakyamuni's only son.

Shakyamuni noticed that his daily conversations with his wives tended to be very mundane, and he wondered why his wives talked so much about gossip. He was also exhausted by the jealousy and possessiveness between them. This sort of environment made it extremely difficult for him to meditate and immerse himself in philosophical contemplation. Thus, he yearned to be alone, and this desire eventually grew very strong in him.

What's more, apart from these women, he was also surrounded by many attendants. Every decision he made required their acknowledgement, and every time he wanted to do something, he had to be accompanied by them. Thus, he earnestly longed to find solitude away from the palace for the chance to reflect within himself.

In addition to these three main reasons, there was a social custom in Shakyamuni's time that was similar to the idea behind studying abroad or moving to a big city. In those days, India allowed those who had provided an heir and who possessed sufficient wealth to secure their family's livelihood to become ascetics.

The Search for a Teacher

Since many biographies describe the people Shakyamuni met after setting off from the palace and how he went through ascetic discipline, it is well-known that, after leaving the royal palace at the age of twenty-nine, he began wandering the country in search of a teacher. The journey of his search and all the austerities he went through were not in vain. They contributed to his spiritual growth and gave him an important chance to observe first-hand the lives of the ascetics and to understand what they were seeking. What he discovered about them can be summarized in two main points.

First, the worship of superhuman abilities was widespread in India at the time, and people yearned to attain a state beyond ordinary human capabilities. Many people wanted to find some way of escaping the suffering of this world. Second, he observed that many people were seeking the principles of happiness in life and trying to explain their own way of achieving it.

One teacher taught that torturing the body was the

shortest way to enlightenment. He believed that the less the mind thought about the things associated with the physical body, the closer the person would come to enlightenment. To practice his teaching, the people who followed him walked on fire, meditated in a cross-legged position underwater, stood on their heads, cut and pierced their bodies with blades and needles, and so on.

Another teacher concentrated on stopping thought. He reasoned that the source of life's difficulties was the thoughts that pass through the mind. Therefore, he was convinced that all worries would disappear if people could stop thinking and find the supreme joy of tranquility. This was where the idea of the "meditation to think nothing" originated.

Yet another teacher was immersed in debating skills and thought that enlightenment was about winning arguments. He focused on ways of eluding verbal assaults, rather than on clearly defining what enlightenment was.

After spending some time with these teachers, Shakyamuni couldn't help but feel that something important was missing from their thinking. He came to the conclusion that what they taught lacked actual teachings. No matter how hard he tried to find the answers, no one was able to explain the essence of enlightenment, the purpose of life, or the spiritual essence of humans. So, less than a year after his renunciation of secular life, he stopped searching for a teacher. Instead, he decided to look to his own mind as his teacher and began seeking a way to find Eternal Buddha, or God, within himself. The goal of his ascetic training was now to discover the Laws of Truth.

The Ascetic Life

In Shakyamuni's resolve to find enlightenment on his own, he went into the forest to be quietly by himself. There, he pondered, and pondered some more, in pursuit of a method that worked. Sometimes he would contemplate in a part of the forest infested by poisonous snakes. Or he would meditate at dawn on the banks of the Nairanjana River. He spent some nights wide-awake because he couldn't sleep, and then he continued his meditation in broad daylight, with perspiration streaming from his body. He didn't stop there. He continued in deep thought as he gazed at a leaf, meditated in a cave, or watched the flowing ripples of a river. Quietly and silently, he persisted in his pursuit of the way to attain enlightenment.

During his search for a teacher, two famous hermits had taught him about the importance of concentrating the mind through meditation. They were Alara-Kalama, who taught meditation in the state of nothingness, and Udraka-Ramaputra, who taught meditation in a state in which neither thought nor no-thought existed.

While their method of meditation helped Shakyamuni develop the ability to achieve peace of mind, he was in search of more than just a way to attain a state of mind. He was in pursuit of Truth, which was theoretical by nature. He had left them for this reason—to find higher wisdom beyond just the practice of meditation. Thus, when he began ascetic training by himself, he started with the objective of withdrawing himself from worldly troubles and so chose to live in remote places away from the villages.

As he tried to eliminate all the worldly desires from his mind, the one desire that caused him the most struggle was hunger. The lack of food exacerbated his urge to search for something he could eat. This experience taught him that when one of the human desires grows exceptionally intense, the strength of the other ones diminishes significantly. For example, when he spent several days without food, his hunger grew so strong that his desires of lust and sleep gradually faded. But he also learned that, no matter how long he immersed himself in ascetic discipline, the desires themselves never completely disappeared.

As he continued living on what he could find in the woods, such as berries and leaves, for sustenance, his physical strength dwindled. His legs weakened so much that he began to spend most of his time sitting in meditation in a cave.

Self-Reflection

Several years passed this way. Shakyamuni spent most of the hours of each day in a cave, except for the few hours when he would go into the forest to find food. During this period of ascetic living, he contemplated deeply the following questions: "What is the purpose of life? Why are we born into a world afflicted by incessant war? Does the path to becoming an awakened one, which so many people are trying to teach, truly lead to the attainment of happiness? So many people despair of war and renounce secular life, but what have they reaped from this? Have they found enlightenment? Have they found liberation from suffering, upon death, and attained bliss in the other world? No one has ever been able to answer these questions for sure. Are they living in an illusion?"

He also reflected deeply on himself: "Several years have already gone by since I left Kapilavastu. I wonder how my father and stepmother, King Shuddhodana and Mahaprajapati, and my attendants are doing. Yashodhara, my wife, must be in such sadness. I wonder, also, how my only son, Rahula, is doing. I renounced my worldly duties and abandoned family ties in pursuit of enlightenment, but will I ever be able to reach it? Is it even attainable? Since I left the palace, have I gotten any closer to enlightenment, grown in character, or gained a deeper understanding of the purpose and mission of life?"

No matter how hard he tried to banish his worldly desires, his fixation on them only grew. The more he tried to erase his family and relationships from his mind, the more concerned he became about them. Then, he noticed the sound of the water dripping from the ceiling of his cave. He looked at himself and saw his body reduced to skin and bone, and he reflected deeply on whether this was really the right way to search for enlightenment.

With these doubts gnawing at his mind, he wondered how much longer his determination to carry on by himself would last. Over and over, these doubts would rise in his mind, and he would wonder whether it was time to go back to the palace. But these thoughts would then fade into unconsciousness. He struggled many days in this state of mind.

The Village Girl

One day, Shakyamuni decided to leave his cave at Gayasisa (or Elephant Head Peak) near Gaya, the capital of the ancient kingdom of Magadha, and went toward the River Nairanjana. In the Uruvilva-Senani village along the river, he began a new phase of his discipline. The scenic surroundings of the village, now known as Sujata, were an ideal place for his discipline. The breezes were refreshing, the forest was beautiful, and the river was crystal clear. He often went to the river to bathe, but his body had grown so thin that the currents nearly carried him away.

One day, he noticed a village girl singing on the other side of the river. He was captivated by her voice. Her voice evoked nostalgic memories of human society, but it was also music from heaven to his ears. She was singing a traditional Indian folk song about a musical instrument that was similar to a lute. The song went: "The strings of the lute will snap when they are pulled too tight. But the sound is too dulled when they are loosened too far. The most beautiful melodies are created when the strings are tuned moderately tight. Dance and dance to the sound of the strings. Let's dance and dance to the sound of the strings."

When he saw the singing girl, he realized in astonishment how haggard he looked compared with her. To his eyes, she looked like an angel with flaxen hair and sparkling eyes. She brimmed with vitality and exuded a lovely fragrance, almost out of keeping with her humble standing as a village girl. In contrast, his body was reduced to skin and bone. His eyes were so sunken, and his ribs protruded so prominently, that he now resembled a skeleton. He was still thirty-five, but anyone would have thought that his death was imminent.

When she caught sight of Shakyamuni, she ran to him from across the bridge, introduced herself as Sujata, and offered him a bowl of milk porridge. The moment he tasted the porridge, he felt hot tears streaming from his eyes. Although it was a humble dish, the porridge tasted heavenly to him, who had been surviving on berries and grass roots until now.

His tears came from the shame he felt for shunning the joys of life so strongly and from realizing the futility of ascetic discipline. He realized, "What beauty is there to a life of ascetic discipline, if I am only reduced to skin and bones and my life is cut short? How much value can there be to such a life? Sujata may never have even given a thought to enlightenment. She may never have studied anyone's teachings or gone through ascetic discipline. But how is she so radiant? She is full of heavenly light." The difference between them, he now realized, was ultimately the difference between someone with the will to live and another who was seeking death.

When he thought of the tears that ran down his cheeks, he was surprised to find that he still had tears to cry. But he also realized how miserable and lonely it is to have a heart that seeks death. Shakyamuni's encounter with Sujata, at the age of thirty-five and several months, was the beginning of the next phase of his life.

6 The Will to Live

The encounter with Sujata made Shakyamuni realize how much he needed to rebuild his strength. The tears that he shed may have been his heart's farewell to the past. The milk porridge tasted rich and delicious, and he felt an indescribable sense of vitality awaken in him as it slowly reached his stomach. He now understood that the denial of food did not necessarily lead to Truth. He realized, also, that the vegetables must also be delighted to be valued and to be providing nourishment and energy and not to be going to waste.

He thought, "In the end, all things in this world exist to serve and be used as ingredients for a higher purpose beyond themselves. It is arrogant for us to shun these ingredients and deem them meaningless. If vegetables are left as they are, they might not produce anything we value. But if we cook them, they can become a delicious meal. This is something that heaven would wish us to do." He firmly resolved to change his life. He determined to start over and transform himself. The tears that streamed down his cheeks, the warmth and strength of the food that filled his stomach, and the radiant vitality of Sujata, all helped him embark on this new stage.

Sujata's song had also powerfully inspired him. There was a phrase that left an especially deep impression on him: "The most beautiful melodies are created when the strings are tuned moderately tight." Shakyamuni thought to himself, "This is right. The answer that I needed is to tune the strings moderately tight. Pull them too tightly, and they will snap in half. Loosen them too far, and they will fall out of tune or become too loose to create sound. The state that I am in right now is probably like the string that was pulled too tightly. I am bound to break at the slightest touch. I wouldn't be able to play any beautiful songs in such a state. So far, I have been too proud of my extreme discipline. Now, I see that this kind of life pales compared with even the ordinary, everyday life of a young village girl. If both of us stood at the door to heaven now, I don't doubt that it would open for her, but it might not allow me through. I am in such a haggard state right now, as if I had just come out of hell. If only I have the chance to live a little longer—even just a few more years—I will restore strength to my body and search for the true meaning of life. I will search until I find the positive purpose of this world."

This was the moment that he reawakened his will to live. This may have also been the very first step he took toward enlightenment. He now understood that enlightenment cannot be achieved through extreme ascetic discipline. That way of life would only lead him to death. And what meaning would there be to being born into this world if the purpose of life was to seek death?

So, he put his palms together in a prayer-like gesture and bowed to Sujata to express his gratitude. He bid her farewell and set out on his way. As he walked on, he noticed that life was everywhere. All the grasses, flowers, and trees were exuding vivacity. They had always been around him, but he had been so immersed in his discipline that he had never noticed all the vitality that surrounded him.

He contemplated, "If even a single flower on the edge of the path were to keep wishing for death to permanently escape from this world, what would become of this world? What would happen if all the animals loathed their lives and wished to die as soon as possible? What if the cows and horses refused to eat? What would happen if they refused to give birth to offspring?"

Peace of Mind

Consequently, Shakyamuni decided to begin accepting offerings of food. He remained in the grove of Uruvilva. And twice a day—early in the morning and again in the afternoon—he made regular rounds to the villagers' houses to gather alms with gratitude.

As soon as he decided to start accepting these alms, he began to feel peace and harmony filling his mind. Before, he had been so intent on practicing discipline on his own—whether it was in collecting food or something else—that he had refused to accept help from others. But now he realized that that way of thinking was just like the over-tightened lute. So he reminded himself to practice moderation. Since, as an ascetic, he could not change the fact that he had no means of subsistence, he decided to accept his situation. He stopped straining himself, trying to be pretentious, and trying to fool himself into thinking that he was not hungry. In addition, giving alms was a valued custom in India that enabled pious lay people to create reserves of virtuous acts in heaven. These were the reasons why he decided to receive alms and spend however much remained of his life in wholehearted pursuit of enlightenment.

When he stopped constantly thinking, "By myself," the overexertion and tension of trying to be independent diminished. He was able to relax and smile again. And as his body regained flesh, he felt energy and vitality gradually return. How unconfident, passive, and full of negative thoughts he had been!

Another change he noticed was that being relaxed gave him room in his heart to consider the people around him. He was now inspired with new aspirations: "I want to learn about all kinds of people and be able to offer them good advice. Not only that, but I should also develop the ability to make the right decisions about myself. In order to do that, I want to achieve and experience enlightenment, which so many ascetics are seeking. And, once and for all, I would like to find out the purpose of life and the meaning of this world. Some day, I shall come to know what it means to be an awakened one—a Buddha—and experience for myself what it is like to live such a life. This is what I want to achieve."

He heard his inner voice saying, "Say farewell to the old way of life, and begin your new journey." It no longer mattered where he lived, since he was now accepting alms for his sustenance. He was no longer restricted to places where berries and edible roots could be found. Therefore, he set off on a new journey. In pursuit of enlightenment, he went wherever he pleased, for this was his chance to see the world and be in touch with people's hearts. Several days later, he arrived in a town called Gaya.

The Confrontation with Evil Within

Gaya was a town of considerable size: it housed several thousand townspeople. There was a group of shops in the center, and the streets bustled with passersby. It was probably large enough to be considered a city by the standards of Shakyamuni's time.

Not far from a river, he found a large pipal tree (also known as an asvattha) so vast that two people could not encircle its trunk with their arms. It provided good shelter from the wind and rain and offered the perfect spot for his meditation. Each day, during the day, he went to the town to gather alms and offerings. Then he returned to the tree to spend the hours from dusk till dawn immersing himself in his quest for enlightenment.

He concentrated mainly on self-reflective meditation. He had learned before that trying to focus his mind on a single thought with his eyes closed tended to invite disruption by evil spirits. So to achieve harmony of mind, he instead reflected upon the things he had thought and done since he was a small child. If he recalled situations when he had gone against his conscience, he repented them. However, as he reflected on the years of his late twenties, he encountered a thought that caused him to struggle. No matter how deeply he reflected, he could not find a solution to stop it from reappearing.

It was the thought of his wife Yashodhara and his son, Rahula. Their faces haunted him. He constantly wondered how big his son must have grown by now. And when he thought of his wife, his heart ached for the deep sadness she must be going through. He just could not stop the pain in his heart.

By this time, a small window into his mind had started to open, and he could hear the voices of beings from the spirit world. One day, while he was sitting in meditation under the pipal tree, a voice began speaking to him from within his mind.

This voice said to him, "I am Brahma. I have come to speak to you. You have spent six years in search of enlightenment, but how much have you achieved from this search? In the end, haven't you only proved that you are an ordinary person? Haven't you forgotten to fulfill the basic duties of a person? You are supposed to find a wife, have children, raise a family, and live happily with them. This is everyone's basic responsibility. But look at yourself. You abandoned your family and gave up happiness just to meditate beneath a tree. What meaning does this have in your life? This was a complete mistake. You must return to your wife and son in the palace. They will be overjoyed at your return, and the path to a great enlightenment will begin for you.

"Just think: how will you have any joy in the other world if you have not lived with joy in this world? You must seek all the pleasure that you can in this life. Your aim should be to enjoy your life to the fullest. The greater the joy you achieved here, the greater the happiness you will reap in the other world. You should admit that you have not had much joy so far. So return, and be with your family, and find happiness with them. Live with them in luxury. This is the spiritual purpose of your life."

There was some truth in what this voice said. And it had pointed out Shakyamuni's biggest soft spot. He deeply regretted the hurt he must be causing his wife, and he still had strong affection for his father, stepmother, and all those who raised him so lovingly. No matter how long he repented for deserting them and being a terrible son, husband, and father, the pain in his heart did not disappear. There was nothing he could do. His self-doubt was swaying his determination, and he wondered whether he really should return to the palace and succeed his father to the throne.

Nonetheless, something about what the voice said did not sound right. The voice said that the more he enjoyed this world, the more pleasure he would have in the next life. It sounded plausible, but he saw that something was slightly wrong with this logic—that the voice was carefully glossing over something important. He realized that his attachment to this world, still deep inside him, was being brought to light, and that the being that called itself Brahma was actually the devil. Shakyamuni said sternly, "You must be a devil. You called yourself Brahma, but you are most definitely not. Admit that you are really a spirit who deludes many spiritual seekers. You are Mara Papiyas the devil; you cannot deceive my eyes." The moment he said this, the voice changed into high-pitched laughter. "Ha-ha-ha! Well done. You saw through my deception. I'll give it to you that you've come this far in your training. Go on with your ascetic training, and live the futile life you so desire!"

Through this confrontation, Shakyamuni discovered that the devil actually existed within his own mind. He wasn't being tempted and deceived by a devil from the outside. The devil had only been attracted by Shakyamuni's own weakness or obsession, which had developed into an attachment of the mind. Thus, he realized that true peace of mind is achieved by letting go of these attachments. Even the most natural affection for his wife, son, father, and mother, if it persisted and became obsessive, would cause him to suffer. The devil had used this very soft spot to make its way into his mind.

Shakyamuni realized that getting rid of the attachments of the inner world was the first step of his new training and that this was different from just giving up the desire to eat or being satisfied with humble food and clothing.

9 The Great Enlightenment

As a result of Shakyamuni's confrontation with the devil Mara Papiyas, he learned that any worldly desire could be an invitation to devils. His self-reflective meditation deepened further: "In the depths of the inner world and in the recesses of the subconscious, the guardian and guiding spirits of heaven are not the only beings that are there. Devils are also lurking within us. They find the dark thoughts that lie in a person's mind and feed on them for energy. And whenever there is a chance to catch the person off guard, they will take control of the mind and begin manipulating it to their own advantage."

Then he reached an enlightenment: "When the mind becomes too focused and affixed to one thought—whether good or bad—it loses freedom and purity and turns into pain. This is what the devils like to target. Therefore, we must allow our thoughts to flow freely through the mind like a stream without obstruction. This freedom from attachment is the state of mind we should all seek. Thus, I need to end any sense of obligation and allow my mind to be free, open, rich, and peaceful."

He continued to reflect on his whole life of nearly thirty-six years. He discarded any negative thoughts that obsessed his mind, and in so doing, he became free of attachment. A great sense of peace enveloped him. How completely different this felt from the encounter with the devil! He felt the warmth of heavenly light flowing into his chest, and it was in this moment that he truly heard the voice of Brahma.

Shakyamuni heard the voice say, "We are overjoyed that you have at last attained enlightenment. We have been watching over you for a long time and waiting for this moment to come. You have achieved the first step of enlightenment. Without this enlightenment, you could not fulfill your mission in this life. We watched in concern when you became immersed in luxury and worldly pleasures. We also watched over you with trepidation when you began the ascetic life. You could have died from malnutrition or committed suicide. Despite it all, you have overcome these obstacles, and your mind has reached us and opened to our voices. We are truly delighted."

In fact, these voices belonged to his brother souls who had incarnated in the past as Rient Arl Croud, Hermes, and others. But they called themselves by a name familiar to Indian culture, Brahma, to avoid confusing him.

From then on, his enlightenment grew ever deeper into an ability to see the past, present, and future. His inner eye penetrated the secrets of the origin of the universe, the birth and history of the Planet Earth, the rise and fall of civilizations, his own previous incarnations, and the future of humanity. When his mind found peace and freedom from attachment, he felt his spiritual body expanding to become as big as the universe, leaving his physical body behind, beneath the pipal tree. This experience is unique to those who have unlocked the door to their inner kingdom, and it is proof that he had fully attained complete liberation of the soul. In short, his full realization that the soul and the physical body are not the same marked the very first step of his great enlightenment.

The Beginning of His Mission

In this chapter, I have explored Shakyamuni's inner journey to his first enlightenment beneath the Bodhi tree, the moment that he awakened and became the person we know as the Buddha. He wished he could bask in this state of the highest enlightenment forever. But those who have experienced enlightenment know that the ordinary, everyday life always returns.

And now that he had savored the enlightenment that so many people sought, he was eager to convey what he had understood to as many people as possible, as quickly as he could. He felt that to keep this wisdom to himself would defeat the purpose of his life. So when he went to gather alms, he also took every opportunity he could find to share his experience with the townspeople and let them know that he was the awakened one.

Many people did not believe him in the beginning. Many thought he had gone crazy and was arrogant to think that he had been able to attain enlightenment on his own. But he could not contain the extraordinary happiness he felt, and he set out to look for the five ascetics who were training with the teacher Udraka-Ramaputra. When they saw that Shakyamuni had reached the same level of enlightenment as their teacher in such a short time, they decided to follow Shakyamuni. This was how he began to preach his wisdom.

His teachings would spread far and wide, but this worldwide influence first began with one thought: his desire to impart the wisdom he had gained from his experience. He especially wished for other ascetic seekers to understand it for themselves. This marked the beginning of his mission to preach the Truths, and this moment later came to be known as the First Turning of the Dharma Wheel. As he thought to himself of future generations who would remember this important day, he felt his heart race with joy and strength surge through his veins. With both the urge to preach the Truths and the desire to continue his inner journey coursing through his body, he could not sit still for even one more day.

THE EIGHTFOLD PATH

The Essence of the Eightfold Path

When Shakyamuni achieved enlightenment, he had already conceived the essence of one of his most famous teachings: the Eightfold Path. With more time, he was able to develop this wisdom into a practice that he could teach to others. For a year, he continued to deepen this idea and devoted himself to developing a teaching that couldn't be learned from other teachers, and to finding a way to reach people's heart with his enlightenment.

Through conversations with his disciples and others around him, he realized that the key was to find a simple guide to convey his wisdom. After deep contemplation, he reached the conclusion that the essence of his enlightenment was to restore our "right" mind—the authentic state of the mind. Then, he considered: how do we go about returning to the right state of mind? As we live our daily lives, many thoughts swim through the mind, and we are apt to lose sight of who we really are, what we think, and what lies deep within our mind. From pride or an inferiority complex, there are times when we try to put on an act for others. So what must we do to fine-tune the inner world? He discovered that, ultimately, this fine-tuning is achieved by a deep self-reflection through the pure eye of Eternal Buddha, or God, within us. He called this heavenly part of us the "divine nature" or "true self."

With the help of a retreat from the energy and attention of the world around us, everyone is capable of looking within the heart and baring the honest and true self. Our candid thoughts are able to come to clear light as we sit alone with ourselves in quiet meditation. This is when the authentic mind wakes up and the impartial eye of Eternal Buddha within judges our thoughts and actions. The starting point of the Eightfold Path was the practice of self-reflection with this pure eye.

Shakyamuni took the eight things we do and the ways we direct our thoughts in daily life—seeing, thinking, speaking, acting, living, making effort, using the will, and meditating—and developed them into specific goals of the Eightfold Path. Then he used the word "right" to describe these goals. But he did not mean "right" as opposed to "wrong." By a "right" thought or action, he was describing the practice of deep introspection, which leads us to Right View, Right Thought, Right Speech, Right Action, Right Livelihood, Right Effort, Right Mindfulness, and Right Concentration. This became his basic method of self-reflection. He usually spent about twenty minutes on each one and frequently chose to meditate in the tranquility of the evenings or at the break of day. With each self-reflection, he felt his heart getting lighter and purer with each passing day.

The Mystical Power of Self-Reflection

Now we have a brief overview of this method of self-reflection. Next, we may wonder why Shakyamuni made this a key teaching. What purpose did he give self-reflection? Self-reflection is an essential way of returning heavenly light to the inner self. In other words, this practice restores the radiance we originally possessed in heaven.

And he had in mind a particular place in heaven. There are many worlds called "dimensions" there that are stacked upon one another, beginning with the fourth dimension and rising to the ninth. Ultimately, he taught self-reflection to elevate us to the radiance of the angels and bodhisattvas in the seventh dimension, where the brilliance of a soul begins to truly manifest. This is a world of souls who are concentrating on helping others through their work. But to reach their brilliance, your mind must first be cleaned of the dust and grime that are casting a shadow over your inner light. When the haze is gone, your true radiance will be set free, and control of your inner world will be restored.

Only then are you ready to move on to the next step of helping others.

Let me explain these steps with examples from daily life. You wouldn't want to use a dirty dishcloth to wipe your dishes. You would make sure that your dishcloth has been laundered before you use it. The same can be said about the mop you use to clean your floors. Attempting to scrub the floor with a dirty mop will only result in spreading more dirt and grime onto it. By the same token, you won't make a good impression, no matter how well-dressed and put together you appear on the outside, if you have not changed your undergarments for many days. And the zealous effort of a teacher will be in vain if he has not educated himself about what he is teaching his students. Altruistic intentions tend to come rather naturally to us. But it requires inner cultivation for these intentions to produce actual altruistic acts. This is why the first step—cleaning our own mind and restoring its original brilliance—is so essential. The fact that this is possible is the miracle of self-reflection.

At the very least, we are given full autonomy over our own state of mind. So before we try to help others clean their mind and reclaim their inner light, we need to restore spiritual light to our own soul. We need to have first-hand experience in feeling the weight lift away and sensing the mind shining to be able to understand and teach self-reflection. This attitude, I believe, is fundamental for those who want to learn the Laws of Truth.

In a narrow interpretation, what I have said may seem as though I am solely encouraging the pursuit of self-interest. But what I am trying to point out is the value of cultivating ourselves, not the value of egotistical living. If an aspiration for self-growth is missing, the teachings will have no power on this person. I would like to emphasize that our ability to comprehend the Laws of Truth begins with achieving inner self-mastery for ourselves.

3 Right View

The first step of the Eightfold Path is to reflect on Right View. To practice Right View is to use the eye of your inner wisdom to impartially review the perceptions you are holding onto. Through my own practice of self-reflection, I have come to see that the majority of life's problems originate from our physical sight. It is the things we see that most often stir up our desires. If we were blindfolded, we would have fewer chances to make mistakes in life. For example, it is impossible to curb the pangs of hunger we feel at the sight of a sumptuous meal. When we notice beautiful jewelry adorning someone's outfit, we feel an urge to run to the mall. And seeing a beautiful woman or a charmer give you a smile is certain to inspire daydreams throughout the day. The swelling desires and emotions that we feel are, more often than not, elicited by the sights that surround us. The key to reflecting with a Right View, then, is to sieve through the perceptions that have swept into the mind through the eyes.

A relaxed mind is essential to this type of deep introspection. If you feel tension in your heart or body at the end of the day, begin by calming your breathing and allowing your mind to follow. Allow your consciousness to descend far down into the inner world. The moment will come when you begin to feel the light pouring in from above and filling you with sublime energy. In this moment, you have become connected to and are at one with Eternal Buddha (God).

Your mind is now ready to examine your day from this higher perspective. This practice resembles the way a detached observer analyzes someone else's perceptions. As I have said, the practice of a right view of our lives ultimately boils down to how we choose to perceive the situations that happen around us. Everything can be seen from different angles, and there are many interpretations to choose from. For example, suppose a new recruit has made a proposal about a general management strategy for your company. People often take different positions on this type of situation. You would have the choice to consider his enthusiasm either positively or negatively. If you evaluated him positively, you might say that he is an enthusiastic and progressive-minded employee with a future full of promise. If, on the other hand, you chose a negative view of him, you might judge him for being pretentious and speaking prematurely before he has had a chance to develop basic skills.

Which of these views is closer to the truth? If you

took the latter view, but concluded that the former was the better perspective, then you would need to consider why you initially took the latter view. What could have caused you to harbor ill feelings toward this person? You might realize that your emotion traces back to criticisms you received in a similar situation when you were new to the job. Or you might discover that it is a reflection of a self-loathing for your inability to speak out and express your opinions. By asking yourself these questions, you can bring to light the root cause of your negative reaction and clear out the gloom within your mind.

In the traditional Buddhist sense, Right View can also be practiced with the Four Noble Truths (the Truth of Suffering, the Truth of the Cause, the Truth of Extinction, and the Truth of the Path). Right View can also be practiced by contemplating causes and effects, based on the teaching of the law of causality.

Right Thought

The next step of the Eightfold Path is Right Thought. The goal of this step is to examine whether your thoughts are aligned with the Truths. By Truths, I mean the same thing as Eternal Buddha's way of thinking. Needless to say, it is a challenge to put yourself in His position to assess each of your thoughts objectively. But thoughts are the most predominant part of the mind—so much so that 70 to 80 percent of self-reflection will be completed by mastering our thoughts alone. Indeed, the human mind is capable of thoughts too numerous to describe and they vary widely from person to person. But all thoughts are the meandering abstractions that we have throughout the day. And like the waves of the ocean, they may pass through the mind quite aimlessly, sweeping in and rolling out without a clear destination.

We are actually the result of these thoughts we have day in and day out. Therefore, what other way to self-growth can there be, than to transform our thoughts into the purest and highest that is possible? We can understand who someone is by looking at the thoughts that are dominating their inner world. However, it is possible for us to live with peace of mind because no one can peek into our minds. Our actions are the sole means by which others can understand what kind of person we are. But what if, by a miracle, there were a door into your mind that could be opened with a key? With the turn of a key, anyone could look into your mind and watch your thoughts appear on a screen like a television show. In an instant, your viewers would know what kind of person you have been. If the screen showed an array of debris, it would reveal that you had been living a disappointing life. But if it showed beautiful thoughts instead, it would reveal that your life had been truly wonderful.

Ultimately, we alone are capable of discerning what is in our own mind and cultivating it to a higher plane. And this is where we must begin. And by so doing, we are also contributing to the beautification of this world. The greater the number of people who clean their minds and beautify the thoughts they send out, the closer the world rises toward heaven, and the further it is removed from hell.

It is a good habit to bring your attention to the images and ideas in your mind now and then throughout the day. Then, when you notice a wrong thought sweep through you, grab the chance to make amends immediately. In your mind, say, "I'm sorry for having this negative thought."

Besides this, I also recommend spending some time at the close of each day to reflect on the thoughts that you had. For example, you might consider the question, "Did I speak unkindly of anyone?" If you did not, then you deserve to be proud of yourself. If, on the other hand, you stopped yourself just before a negative remark slipped from your lips, you may have practiced Right Speech. But what about your thoughts? If your thoughts were still filled with resentment, then clearly, these feelings should be amended. By continuing in this way, through the power of habit and consistency, your self-reflection will steadily deepen and you will gain control over your thoughts.

It should be noted that Right Thought is explained in traditional Buddhism as having the proper aspirations in spiritual practice and making the right judgments on daily matters based on the Truths.

Right Speech

The third step in the Eightfold Path is to review how well you have practiced Right Speech. As you've probably noticed, Right View is vital to the health of the mind because poisons are formed by the wrong perspectives. In the same way, Right Speech prevents poisons from seeping into the mind, as well as traveling and spreading to others.

Spoken words are so potent that the majority of the problems of life find their roots in them. Someone's words can make us feel unhappy, while it's just as likely for something we say to cause someone else pain. Thus, words and happiness have an inseparable relationship. It isn't an exaggeration to say that if everyone in the world could speak well-tuned words, this world will transform into heaven on Earth.

Let's consider the words that are spoken in heaven. The words of those in heaven are beautifully well-tuned. The more accomplished they are in this art, the closer they live to the divine spirits. The divine spirits never speak malicious words. They may occasionally make critical remarks, but these always come from their love—never hatred—and an intention to direct someone to a higher virtue.

By imagining the conversations of heaven, it is easy to see that spoken words are a telling representation of inner character. Therefore, reflecting on your words is an essential as well as a straightforward element of practicing self-reflection. For example, when you reflect on Right Speech today, you can begin by recalling each of the moments in which you expressed your thoughts. If you find this difficult to do, you can make it easier by remembering the people you met throughout the day, since all your words were spoken to someone.

Consider your words one by one, and examine what you expressed. When we are stressed, dealing with a problem, or not feeling our best physically, we are prone to saying negative words. Negative words are the things we say that do not bring happy feelings to anyone. They tend to impart hurt, anxiousness, and despair. These words resemble a contagious disease that reproduces and spreads unhappy thoughts and feelings to those around us. Everyone has their bad days, and that's harmless when we keep our gloom to ourselves. But by allowing our negative feelings to come through in the things we say, we may also ruin someone else's day, and that person may pass the negativity on to someone else.

Therefore, Right Speech is a vital spiritual practice. By fine-tuning our verbal expressions every day to produce good and righteous words aligned with Eternal Buddha's will, we will get better at self-reflection. Eventually, we will progress so far that our introspection will reach the very roots of our words: our thoughts.

More specifically, the goal of Right Speech is to always speak honestly and avoid complaining, lying, flattering, and deceiving.

Right Action

Traditionally, Buddhism has explained Right Action as the prohibition of criminal acts, such as killing, stealing, and committing adultery. But, now, these goals may be too basic for modern life. Nowadays, the scale of our economic activity has grown vast and continues to expand, making everyday life much more complex than it used to be. Thus, I believe that Right Action these days includes the actions associated with work. So in this section, I would like to explain Right Action as a way to consider the ideal way of doing one's job.

A discussion of the proper way of working raises an essential point about how we think about a profit-based society. These days, all jobs, whether in business or in public service, are based on profit. Every organization needs to balance its revenue and expenditure to stay alive. Even the public and civil services are using the taxes paid by citizens—profit—to offer them services. Basically, every type of job is expected to produce something of value.

So how should we live in a society like today's? How should we choose our work and perform our jobs with a spiritual point of view? From the perspective of traditional Buddhism, modern society may seem like an impossible place to practice meditation and the Eightfold Path. But I believe in the value that such a society offers to our spiritual growth. The harsh vibrations of a fast-paced world may not be the most favorable for a meditative life. But the soul gains a precious opportunity to further its cultivation and growth.

If we think of Right Action as Right Work, there are two important points to consider. First, your work should be a job that your pure conscience can be happy with. There should also be a feeling in your bones that this is the right work for you. It is my belief that each of us was born with a pre-chosen calling. In the life above, before our journey to the womb, we decided on a plan for this life and resolved to devote ourselves to fulfilling a certain lifework. A job that strays too far from the type of work we chose will make us feel miserable, no matter how well it pays or how much we rely on it for our livelihood. Therefore, it is essential to reflect on whether your current job is aligned with your calling.

To apply this self-reflection to a job within an organization, we should consider whether our job truly suits us. While everyone should be given an equal opportunity, there is no reason for everyone to have the same role. There are different types of jobs within a company for a good reason, and finding the one that suits you well will boost your own performance as well as your company's. It is valuable for the right people to be assigned to the right job. So to live with Right Action, you must first find the vocation that will bring your true potential to life and that will fulfill your life's purpose.

The second essential point of Right Action is to consider whether the purpose of your job will promote your harmony with others and bring happiness to society. I can't emphasize the value of these enough. But then, how should we consider the profits and losses that occur as a result of business competition? Should these be considered evil? Even though competition may seem to create disharmony, it ultimately contributes to the advancement of our society and culture by encouraging the production of new and improved products at lower prices and also prevents monopolization. From the consumer's perspective, it is more desirable to have a variety of options to choose from. So from a broader perspective based on the Truths, the growth that competition contributes to society is a good thing.

Needless to say, it is not right for a job to disrupt the harmony between people. It is just as wrong for businesses to have harmful motives. In whatever work we choose to do, our aim should be to enhance the happiness of others and create positive relationships with society.

Right Livelihood

The fifth step of the Eightfold Path is Right Livelihood. The essence of this step is to consider whether we can be proud of the way we have been leading our life. Being human, we normally don't have trouble finding some aspect of our life that we would like to improve.

This step begins with an appreciation of time. Every person, no matter who it is, is equally granted twenty-four hours in a day and 365 days a year. Not only that, but everyone is also promised a definite conclusion to this life. Even our lifespans don't vary greatly; many of us will be setting off from this world before we reach the age of one hundred. We devote a substantial portion of each day to sleep and spend additional precious hours on meals and other essential activities. The remainder of the day is the precious hours and minutes that remain for our work and free time.

There is something exciting about the fact that each of us was granted the same length of time each day. Time is indeed impartial to all. No matter how talented we were born, our days will never grow or shrink. What matters, then, is the way we use the time we are given. With these twenty-four hours per day, someone will rise into the presidency of the United States, and someone else will become a renowned scholar or a great thinker. And yet, these same twenty-four hours will also result in many jobless lives. When we consider life solely in light of time, we see that these disparities are reflections of how meaningfully we have spent our days.

Therefore, Right Livelihood for modern people is about how valuably we treat each day and each hour. If we take it one step further, we can reflect on longer spans of months and years. But here, I should emphasize an important point. The essence of practicing Right Livelihood is to appreciate time as so fleeting and irretrievable that each day is as precious as a lifetime. We rarely question whether there will be a tomorrow. Just as there was a yesterday and there is a today, we tend to expect tomorrow to come again. We must stop taking each day for granted and remember that there is no guarantee that tomorrow will arrive. So consider: What would you do if you knew that your life would come to a conclusion tonight, let's say at midnight? How would you live the remainder of the day? Would you have any regrets? Like many of us, you would probably have more regrets than you would like.

After all is said and done, Right Livelihood, in a

nutshell, is looking over your life as if today were your very last day and deciding how to spend the hours that have been left to you. Immediately, many of the things you would want to redo, if you had the chance, will dawn on you. So will all the missed opportunities you have let go by. The vital takeaway is this: At the end of every day, reflect on each of your actions, words, and the events of the day as if tomorrow will never come, and consider what your regrets would be. You will live a more meaningful life each day you continue this self-reflection on Right Livelihood.

Finally, I would like to point out that, according to traditional Buddhism, making a living by criminal acts and choosing a vocation that is clearly against the teachings of the Truths—such as working for misleading religions or materialist philosophers—are considered wrong in light of Right Livelihood.

Right Effort

The sixth step is to reflect on the effort we have made so far to live according to the Truths. Unless we make a conscious effort to avoid it, by human nature, we are predisposed to drifting aimlessly from one day to the next. We seem to forget that, regardless of our awareness or lack thereof, the destination of our life has been fixed. Everyone is meant to reach one place at the end of their journey, beyond the gates of death: heaven.

Since the beginning, our goal to return to heaven has been Eternal Buddha's (God's) grand design to keep the soul evolving. Understanding this plan is essential to comprehending the purpose of Right Effort. It explains why we are born into this world—sometimes called the third dimension—and why it exists. It reveals that, ultimately, this world is a training school for the soul. By this, I mean that this life is where we have the chance to practice and refine our understanding of the Truths. Not only that, but this world is His masterpiece of light—enactments of His glory and prosperity. This perspective on life is the key to practicing self-reflection on Right Effort.

There are two essential perspectives that we need to consider in practicing Right Effort. In the first perspective, we must think of this life as the soul's opportunity to experience and learn. Have you ever considered life this way? Have you been making a continuous effort to live with this view of life? If the essence of Right Livelihood is to reflect on our way of life in daily cycles, the essence of Right Effort is to consider our way of life in longer spans of one or more years at a time. Such reflection will help us set middle-term goals in life. What will you do to develop yourself over the next year, the next three years, the next five years, and the next ten years? What do you plan to do in these years for your self-growth?

The second point of view that matters for Right Effort is a spiritual one. In the final analysis, Right Effort is about checking the progress of our spirituality and the height of our spiritual awareness. It does not serve us at all if we are following a way of life that brings decline to the spiritual side of us. Growing our spiritual awareness means, in other words, raising our enlightenment. But what does it mean to raise our enlightenment? And how do we know whether we are making progress? There are three key points to check.

The first point is to be able to see yourself as you are, in the most truthful state. This is the step that engages the detached observer in you—the ability to see from the perspective of Eternal Buddha. When you gain a clear sense of who you are, you are very close to enlightenment. This is the first point you must consider as you examine how close you have come to enlightenment. The second point is to perceive others and yourself not as individuals, but as one grand harmony. You will recognize others as your friends and comrades in mission, all aiming to create the ideal world of light. The third point is to perceive deeply the true purpose of this life and the world around you—to discover the precise meaning of the environment and circumstances that surround you. When these three points show that you have made progress, your spiritual awareness is growing.

Right Mindfulness

The seventh step in the Eightfold Path is Right Mindfulness. The universal custom of prayer is a combination of Right Mindfulness and Right Concentration—the eighth step in the Eightfold Path. Thus, both of these Buddhist practices need to be practiced in prayer. The part of Right Mindfulness that is analogous to prayer is the purposeful energy that we send out to the world. But we must issue this directed thought from inner harmony, and we achieve this through Right Concentration.

In short, to pray is to will for something from a meditative state. Therefore, self-reflection and prayer shouldn't be considered separately; prayer is a component of self-reflection. And supposing this may be theoretically confusing to some, it is just as possible to think of prayer as a dynamic form of self-reflection. But regardless of how it is understood, the heart of the matter is that a part of the Eightfold Path is analogous to prayer.

So how can we direct our thoughts properly? If we

think of practicing Right Thought in terms of how well we control our thoughts, the focus of our concentration in that step is the collection of thoughts that occur within a day. By contrast, the focus of Right Mindfulness is the ideas we have on a much larger scale, including life plans and other visions of the future. What are your goals and plans for the future? What are the accomplishments that you want to achieve? What are the strong wishes you have within your heart?

For example, Right Mindfulness to a homemaker may mean praying for the family's peace and well-being. Right Mindfulness to someone who is dedicated to work may find life to be a constant succession of goals and plans. In a life like this, the kinds of goals and plans we set and the way we direct our mind and energy toward them become vital points of self-reflection.

In short, Right Mindfulness is the practice of directing the will through self-reflection. If, for example, your will is directed toward obstructing someone's happiness or success, that is obviously a wrong use of will. Remember, your thought becomes imprinted in your mind. The goal of this self-reflection should be to wish for the happiness and success of all.

Since the will becomes stronger as we gain the ability to concentrate the mind, our ability to control it becomes all the more essential. However, for those who have never given thought to how we direct our thoughts and never experienced the mystical power of the mind, Right Mindfulness is a very distant goal. In this sense, this is a highly advanced method of self-reflection.

Right Concentration

Last but not least, I would like to briefly explain how to reflect on the eighth step of the Eightfold Path: Right Concentration. This step is, in fact, deeply associated with the heart of religion. The aim of religion, ultimately, is to attune the mind to Eternal Buddha (God) and divine spirits in heaven. By directing the mind to Him and divine spirits, we are able to connect our heart with His and capture what He is feeling.

In this sense, Right Concentration is essential for all who want to awaken their spirituality and experience the universe in a true sense. It can be difficult to advance your meditation enough to discover your past or future lives. But I am certain that, when you descend deeply into the mind, you will begin to receive the inspiration of divine spirits. You will be amazed by this mystical experience and the power of your own mind.

In short, the ultimate purpose of Right Concentration is the liberation of the mind from worldly fetters. Through the practice of this self-reflection, your mind will amass true wisdom and the power to achieve emancipation. Another purpose of Right Concentration is the practice of introspection into your inner world. When we keep digging within the mind, we eventually reach a state that can communicate with our guardian and guiding spirits.

In the end, knowledge cannot serve its true purpose unless it has basis in the Truths and regular spiritual practice. This is why Right Concentration is essential even to those who possess a lot of knowledge, no matter how extensive it may be, because neither character nor outstanding spiritual stature can be developed without Right Concentration.

At the same time, there have been many great figures who weren't necessarily immersed in religion. What the majority of them had in common was an appreciation for introspection. They had their own methods of spending time on this, whether it was on walks or in contemplative thinking. In one way or another, each had a way of immersing her mind in Right Concentration and accessing the energy of the grand universe.

Only when we attain Right Concentration does our potential become limitless. No matter who we are, our intellect is enclosed within human limitations. But with Right Concentration, we can break through these walls and open the mind to tap into the wisdom of the whole universe. Therefore, to reflect on Right Concentration is to reflect on how much of the universe we are able to see within us. It is to consider how much we recognize ourselves as a member of and a part of the universe created by Eternal Buddha (God).

Thus, you will complete your spiritual training only when you achieve this state of Right Concentration. When you complete your practice of the Eightfold Path—Right View, Right Thought, Right Speech, Right Action, Right Livelihood, Right Effort, Right Mindfulness, and Right Concentration—you will attain the mind of an arhat. Then the next stage will be an active one: you will be advancing to the state of a bodhisattva. I hope that now, you have a deeper appreciation of the Eightfold Path as a day-to-day practice, a principle of hope, and the basis of your spiritual growth.

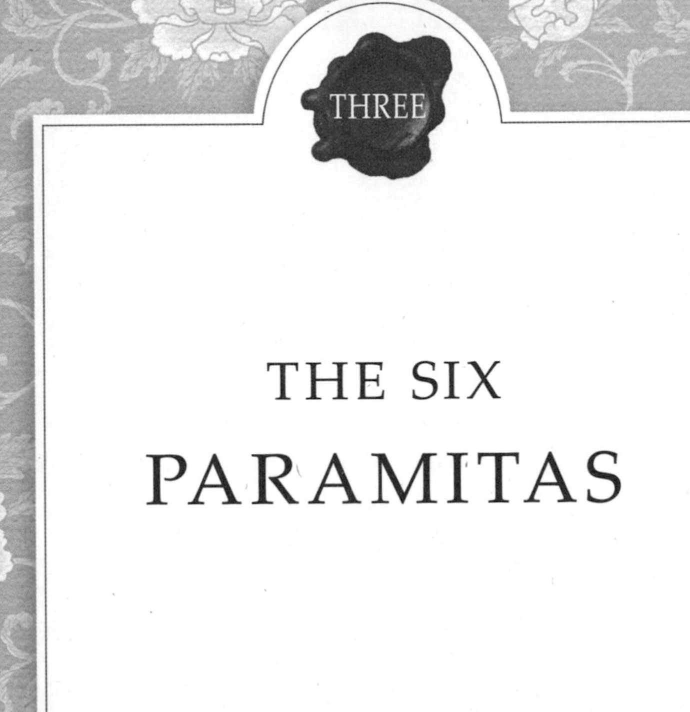

THREE

THE SIX PARAMITAS

Attaining the Innermost Wisdom

If I were to choose an idea that best characterizes Shakyamuni Buddha's teachings, it would be the idea that wisdom exists deep within the mind and wells up like a spring. In contrast to forms of worship that emphasize prayer, Shakyamuni's original teachings were based on a belief in inner power. It should be noted, however, that in later years, as Buddhism became popular and the Mahayana movement began, followers started to worship the Buddha in heaven. This transformation from faith in the power of the self to faith in an outside power was actually supported by Shakyamuni Buddha himself in heaven.

The belief in the power of the self is based on the idea that each and every person has a source of wisdom within that is connected to the will of the universe and to the Primordial Buddha (Primordial God). Shakyamuni's original teaching was a way for an individual to become awakened or to evolve into a Buddha through self-discipline, so at the outset it did not include a belief in a great outside power. Early Buddhism focused on self-discipline, so it did not provide a basis for the worship of an outside power. It is this aspect that distinguishes Buddhism from other religions.

Shakyamuni himself was fully aware of the existence of the Creator of the universe, and he understood the power of divine spirits, for he himself received various forms of guidance from them. However, following the way he had attained enlightenment, Shakyamuni chose to teach his disciples how to go deep into the mind until they reached the wisdom within. The way of reaching deep into the mind to find the innermost wisdom and allowing it to well up is fundamental to Buddhism.

Buddhism and Christianity were taught from two quite different perspectives. Compared with the Christian idea that human beings are born sinful (although this may not have been part of the original teaching of Jesus), Buddhism provides a more advanced way of guiding people to improve themselves. In Christianity, there is no established methodology by which a human being can become closer to God. The existence of God the Father, Christ the Son, and the Holy Spirit is clearly stated, and represented by the theology of the Holy Trinity of the Father, the Son, and the Holy Spirit. However, there is a potential risk of misleading people into believing that they are just like a flock of sheep, eagerly waiting to be saved. That is a sad picture of humanity.

In contrast, the human being that Buddhism describes is much stronger. Buddhism teaches that each and every person has divine nature within. Shakyamuni saw the goodness and the great potential in the essential nature of human beings, and taught that humans are not simply transient physical beings. Although Buddhism teaches ideas that can be interpreted negatively, such as karma, it also teaches the positive concept of an infinite wisdom that exists within the human mind. This positive idea was later developed into the teachings of the Six Paramitas, which consist of the following:

Dana Paramita – the perfection of offering
Sila Paramita – the perfection of observing the precepts
Ksanti Paramita – the perfection of perseverance
Virya Paramita – the perfection of effort
Dhyana Paramita – the perfection of meditation
Prajna Paramita – the perfection of wisdom

Shakyamuni's original teachings were later compiled as the Mahayana philosophy, which holds that as we practice the discipline of the Six Paramitas, our innermost wisdom will well up; that the energy of Eternal Buddha (God) will gush like a fountain. In Mahayana Buddhism, human beings are considered infinitely precious because their essential nature is no different from that of Eternal Buddha.

I hope you will understand that Buddhism, from its

very origin through to its development into a movement of salvation, teaches the positive belief that all people can save themselves or, rather, that everyone is already saved.

Manifesting Thoughts as Deeds

In the previous chapter, I described the Eightfold Path, which focuses on thoughts, the inner activity of human beings. But Shakyamuni did not only see human beings in connection to their inner selves. He also placed great emphasis on the relationship between thought and deed, how the one leads to the other, and whether the two are consistent.

If you really believe something, it will inevitably manifest outwardly. What is deeply inscribed in the mind will inevitably be expressed as action. In the same way, if you seek enlightenment within, what you have understood will be translated into action, and your actions in turn will speak eloquently of the kind of enlightenment you have attained. In reality, thoughts and deeds are not separate; rather, they are like two sides of a coin, so you can check whether you are living rightly, in accordance with the teachings of the Truths, by examining both your thoughts and your actions.

How will your thoughts manifest as action? The Six Paramitas explain how the thoughts that you have refined through the practice of the Eightfold Path are expressed as action. The Eightfold Path and the Six Paramitas may seem to overlap. But if I were to explain the difference, I would say that the Eightfold Path focuses on how to control your thoughts, while the Six Paramitas demonstrate how your thoughts will be expressed in action and how an enlightened person acts.

In the end, you can only determine whether you are seeking Truth rightly by examining both the thoughts within you and the actions that you express outwardly. In Shakyamuni's time in ancient India, it was extremely important to know whether a particular method of self-discipline was right or wrong, and that is still true today. You cannot determine whether a particular religious teaching is right until you have carefully examined the thoughts and actions it teaches. No matter how good the statements of a religious leader may be, his teachings are not worth believing if his character and behavior are questionable. If the core members of an order are totally corrupt, they will not be able to set a good example to seekers of Truth. Seekers of Truth are responsible for proving their ability to control their thoughts through their outer expression—in other words, through actions.

Benefiting the Self Benefits Others

The idea, "benefiting the self benefits others" plays a key role in understanding Shakyamuni Buddha's teachings. Today's Buddhists often say that Mahayana Buddhism did not start until five hundred years after Shakyamuni's death, when seekers formulated the idea of salvation and compiled the Mahayana sutras. One very plausible story tells how Nagarjuna, through astral travel, brought back the entire collection of scriptures from the spirit world and started Mahayana Buddhism based on his experience.

Many people seem to believe that the original teachings of Shakyamuni were the basis of Theravada Buddhism, which focused solely on self-improvement, while Mahayana Buddhism, which focused on the salvation of the masses, was developed centuries after Shakyamuni's death. But this is not true. Of course, many Mahayana sutras were compiled in later years, but Shakyamuni had already taught most of the basic concepts of salvation himself.

Shakyamuni thought, "If refining the self means

living a reclusive life, isolated from society, this sort of effort is in vain. If self-discipline in the search for enlightenment leads only to noble isolation, what is the point of being incarnated on Earth?" When he received an offering of milk porridge from a village girl and ate it, he awakened to the fact that enlightenment was to be found in the Middle Way and understood that extreme asceticism does not lead to spiritual awakening. This idea integrates the concepts of "benefiting the self," which means refining oneself and enhancing a sense of happiness, and "benefiting others," which means sharing this personal happiness with many others.

Human beings are social creatures who cannot live without interacting with others. That is why it is necessary to share with others what you have learned in order to bring them happiness, instead of being conceited about your own abilities. Shakyamuni had all the attributes of a good educator, and his teaching that "benefiting the self benefits others" quite clearly reflects this. This idea can be explained in the following way: at the same time as you make continual efforts to develop and refine yourself, it is important to aim to make this world a better place to live by enlarging the circles of happiness around you and eventually attaining great harmony between yourself and many others. Becoming exceptional must not cause discord with others; instead, your efforts to become an outstanding person must contribute to the happiness of the whole society. In summary, the sense of happiness you achieve by attaining enlightenment should be returned to society and to the people who live in it.

Both "benefiting the self" and "benefiting others" are important ideas, and the order of these two factors is significant. Hidden within this sequence from self-help to helping others is a vital concept connected to seekers' self-discipline.

The self-discipline of the Eightfold Path aims at attaining the state of an arhat of the sixth dimension. If you wish to go beyond this level and attain the state of a bodhisattva of the seventh dimension, it is absolutely necessary to have altruistic thoughts and put them into practice. In other words, the disciplines of self-improvement and altruism should not be separated. In the process of refining yourself, you also have to sow seeds that will grow to benefit others. This is a very important requirement for becoming a bodhisattva. It explains the reason why those who pursued Zen training in an isolated world of self-satisfaction were not able to reach a state beyond that of the sixth dimension.

The teaching of the Six Paramitas is a bridge between the state of bodhisattvas and the state of tathagatas of the eighth dimension. The Six Paramitas are methods that develop the Eightfold Path into guidelines for conduct for those who aim to reach the state of bodhisattvas and beyond. In the following sections, I would like to explain each of the Six Paramitas in detail.

Dana Paramita
(The Perfection of Offering)

The first discipline of the Six Paramitas is Dana Paramita, which is also called the perfection of offering. The teaching of offering is a very important part of Shakyamuni Buddha's teachings. Offering is a Buddhist way of expressing love, and it is similar to the Christian idea of charity. The fact that the perfection of offering is the first discipline of the Six Paramitas shows how much importance Shakyamuni placed on the idea of love or, more specifically, compassion for others.

Now, let me briefly explain the term "Paramita." This Sanskrit word originally meant "reaching the other shore" or "attaining the state of emancipation." It can also be interpreted as "the state in which an abundant wisdom flows out from the well deep within the mind." Thus, Dana Paramita is the discipline of offering, which enables you to fully appreciate and assimilate the wisdom that wells up from within.

There are many different types of offerings. Most common is the offering of material wealth—for instance clothes, property, or precious objects—to mendicant seekers, religious orders, or the poor. Offering is certainly an act of love, and even if you cannot give material things, you can still give a smile. A smile on your face can help make this world a better place in which to live.

Offering the Law or teachings of the Truths is a more advanced, spiritual level of offering. The Law is the best offering for those with a hunger in their soul. Offering the Law is like quenching the thirst of those craving water in a parched desert. In the time of Shakyamuni, lay followers made a habit of offering material goods and food to monks and nuns, and the followers in turn would receive much more than they had given; the mendicants expressed their gratitude to lay followers through their loving act of offering the Law. It was also considered an offering of the Law when lay followers explained the teachings of the Truths to others who were not yet awakened to faith.

Another type of offering is to remove fear from those who are frightened, suffering, or in pain. Removing fear is an offering of peace of mind, because it saves them from the anguish of misfortune. Offering material wealth, offering the Law, and offering peace of mind are called the Three Offerings.

Sila Paramita
(The Perfection of Observing the Precepts)

The next of the Six Paramitas is Sila Paramita, which is also called the perfection of observing the precepts. Many people probably associate self-discipline with following some set of precepts or following a stoic lifestyle. This applies not only to Buddhism but also to other religions. Islam, for example, has extremely strict precepts, and Christianity has a set of rules for the conduct of monks and nuns. The purpose of religious precepts is to protect seekers of Truth from various worldly temptations.

It is not easy for ordinary people to understand what right thought and right action are, so certain guidelines, or the minimum requirements for discipleship, were established as a bulwark against temptations. Shakyamuni regarded the precepts as a very important means of educating people because, unless seekers were given certain rules of conduct, they had difficulty controlling their behavior.

The main requirement of the discipline of Sila Paramita is to observe the following five precepts: do not kill, do not steal, do not commit adultery, do not speak falsely, and do not drink alcohol.

Shakyamuni taught the first precept, not to kill, or the teaching that killing is a sin, because murder was quite common in his time.

Next he taught not to steal. Stealing meant not only taking the possessions of another by force, but also taking things that you were not allowed to possess. An act of stealing may benefit the one who steals, but it causes harm to others, disturbing their peace of mind and creating social disorder. This precept was formulated to avoid this.

The next precept is not to commit adultery. Adultery meant having affairs outside a celebrated marriage. There were two reasons that extramarital affairs were considered wrong. First, these acts destroy the family, which is the basic building block of society. Second, they intensify sensuous desire and thereby prevent the seeker from concentrating on the path to enlightenment. It was for these reasons that this precept was put in place.

In the case of kings and maharajahs, however, having more than one wife was socially acceptable; it was not considered a violation of the precept of not committing adultery. Unlike Christianity, Buddhism did not traditionally stipulate monogamy. As long as a relationship was based on love and sufficient financial support was provided, it was acceptable for a man to have more than one wife to uphold social status. This was actually connected to the fact that Shakyamuni Buddha accepted many members of royal families as his followers.

Next is the precept not to speak falsely. This included telling lies, speaking ill of others, and slandering others. Shakyamuni prohibited his followers from intentionally saying things to frame others. Even within his order, disciples constantly spoke ill of others and envied fellow seekers who had reached advanced levels of enlightenment. These unfortunate circumstances were the grounds for the prohibition of false speech.

The last of the five main Buddhist precepts is not to drink alcohol. Whether drinking alcoholic beverages is good or bad in itself needs to be examined from a different perspective. In fact, some divine spirits in heaven do enjoy the sensation of drinking at times, so the habit of drinking cannot be flatly condemned. However, it should be noted that in Shakyamuni's time, alcohol in India was of very bad quality and caused terrible intoxication, and people at that time generally accepted the idea that drinkers were lazy. In addition, drinking definitely interfered with concentrating the mind and tended to undermine people's desire for self-improvement. The precept against drinking was established to maintain social order. This precept was also set to encourage seekers to continue on the path of self-discipline and to fight worldly temptations and desires.

These were the five precepts that were commonly observed at the time of Shakyamuni. Today, some of these precepts have been instituted as laws, so we may need a different set of precepts for seekers of Truth.

Ksanti Paramita
(The Perfection of Perseverance)

Next comes Ksanti Paramita, which is also called the perfection of perseverance. Following the virtue of offering and the virtue of observing the precepts, Shakyamuni taught the virtue of perseverance.

When you look at Shakyamuni's life, you will see that perseverance played an important role. Perseverance is absolutely essential to the development of the mind and to long-term spiritual improvement. This was the very reason that seekers of Truth were taught the discipline of Ksanti Paramita.

A lack of patience often causes frustration that disturbs peace of mind, and this then gives rise to disharmony in relationships. When you become fully aware that perseverance is the key to victory in life, you will find a new self that has reached an advanced spiritual level.

The discipline of Ksanti Paramita can be summarized in the following four points. The first is a warning against impatience. Seekers of Truth tend to become impatient with their progress; they compare themselves with others and desire to become enlightened before others. However, it takes an extremely long time to attain enlightenment. Because of the very fact that they are seekers, they must endure the pain of not being able to attain enlightenment for a long time. The moment they lose patience, they will begin to stray from the right path.

The second point is tolerance. Tolerance means not only putting up with situations that seem to be against you, but also letting go of feelings of resentment. When we study and practice the teachings of the Truths, we often become subject to criticism and accusations. In fact, the more authentic the teaching, the more intense the enemy attack tends to be. In a world full of wrong thoughts and evil actions, those spreading the Truths often become targets of the forces of evil. When this occurs, seekers must not take in the poison of the attack, but must instead overcome the difficulties quietly and continue to walk steadily on the right path. It is important for seekers to hold on to this attitude.

The third point is endurance in the face of objections from family and relatives. When people decide to walk the path of Truth while living in the material world, it is as if they sever their connection with the past once and for all. After this major turning point, their lives completely change, and those who are close to them may start complaining and try to persuade them to go back on their decision to enter the path of

Truth. Although they do this out of love, it is a worldly love stemming from a lack of more exalted spiritual knowledge. What they think of as "common sense" will inevitably stand in the seeker's way, and it becomes ever more important that seekers endure this hardship and maintain their peace of mind.

The fourth point is endurance of evil. In the process of striving for enlightenment, seekers will have to confront trials put in their way by various evil spirits and devils. Shakyamuni himself was tested by the devil Mara Papiyas, and Jesus was tempted by Beelzebub. In the same way, seekers of Truth cannot avoid the interference of the forces of evil, because the greater the number of enlightened people becomes, the less the territory there is for evil spirits to inhabit. Evil forces, out of an instinct to defend themselves, try to obstruct the forces of light.

It is vital to endure and overcome the enemy attack. The discipline of developing oneself and increasing one's inner light may seem passive, and you may be tempted to try to defeat the devils once and for all. But you should make the effort to persevere, to make it through the challenges you face and finally overcome them. When seekers walk on the path toward the light, they inevitably face trials of darkness before they become truly enlightened, and this is the reason that perseverance is absolutely essential for seekers.

Virya Paramita
(The Perfection of Effort)

Virya Paramita is also called the perfection of effort, and it is the discipline of making effort. The path of Right Effort on the Eightfold Path is essentially the same in concept, but Virya Paramita places more importance on the actual practice of setting a clear objective and working toward it. This discipline requires one to set clear goals and pursue a practice to reach those goals. It requires the accumulation of daily effort to fulfill clear objectives—for example, making offerings, doing meditation, or teaching the Law—in a way that allows others to acknowledge your achievements. If you study the Law, it is also important to assess how much progress you have made every day. The discipline of Virya Paramita is about making concrete efforts, and this was precisely what Shakyamuni's disciples did.

One of the outstanding characteristics of Shakyamuni's order was that its members studied very diligently, and this distinguished them from the followers of other religions. In those days, the worship of supernatural powers was very popular, and a lot of people immersed themselves in demonstrating their extraordinary powers to win respect. Shakyamuni taught his followers how to communicate with the spiritual realms, but at the same time, he expected his followers to possess common sense, to make sound judgments, and to be respected in all walks of society. Thus, members of Shakyamuni's order were strongly motivated and enthusiastic about studying the teachings of the Truths. This strong enthusiasm for learning benefited Shakyamuni's disciples in their efforts to build a balanced foundation of knowledge based on the Truths and to develop their characters.

It is often said that those who continue to study will eventually acquire great stature. In fact, the aim of studying is not only to acquire knowledge; the very process of making a diligent effort to achieve a clear objective in any field of study contributes to the development of character. It is only natural, therefore, that those who diligently study the Truths, the most important of all studies, will refine themselves and become outstanding people.

The virtue of effort was a central part of Shakyamuni's teachings, and any teaching that neglected effort—for example, the idea that anyone can become enlightened without making any effort or the idea that prayer guarantees blessings—was rejected. It should be remembered that Shakyamuni's emphasis on the accumulation of constant effort contributed to raising the level of Buddhist teachings.

Dhyana Paramita
(The Perfection of Meditation)

The discipline of Dhyana Paramita is also called the perfection of meditation. It overlaps with Right Concentration on the Eightfold Path, but the difference between these two types of discipline can be found in their main focus. While Right Concentration emphasizes your state of mind—whether you are reflecting on your thoughts and concentrating your mind rightly—Dhyana Paramita focuses on the virtue of the daily practice of meditation.

When you have spare time, for instance on the weekend, it is probably not so difficult to reflect on yourself and examine your past thoughts and actions. But it is not easy to take the time for self-reflection when you are busy every day. Constantly setting aside time for introspection every day is itself an extraordinary achievement.

I would like you to ponder your own situation. You may not find it difficult to remember what has happened in your life since the time of your birth. But you'll see that it actually takes extraordinary effort to accumulate the effort of discovering, investigating, and checking your inner self on a daily basis.

The ultimate goal of Dhyana Paramita is to be in a constant state of meditation, not only when you are following a formal method of meditation practice, but also during work and other regular activities you engage in every day. In other words, the perfection of Dhyana Paramita means attaining a meditative state no matter what you are doing, whether you are walking, speaking, or working. When you achieve this state of mind, you spend every minute of the twenty-four hours in each day in a state of meditation; your thoughts are constantly directed to the heavenly world, and you can communicate with divine spirits at any time. This is the highest state of mind that seekers of Truth should aim to achieve through their discipline.

Today, followers of Zen Buddhism practice meditation, sitting cross-legged in temples in the remotest places. It is not too difficult to penetrate our inner world deeply when we are detached from our daily lives, but it is extremely hard to maintain a meditative state in our day-to-day work.

When you achieve the highest state of meditation, your mind becomes perfectly calm. Even if someone throws abusive words at you, you will not be affected by the negative energy, and the inner lake within your mind will remain undisturbed and peaceful. When you live with such a perfect state of mind, it will be as if you are living in the heavenly world while still in this world. This is the perfection of Dhyana Paramita that seekers strive to attain. When you achieve this state, your mind will be in the higher dimensions of heaven—the seventh dimension (the World of Bodhisattvas) and the eighth dimension (the World of Tathagatas)—while still living in this physical world. This state was one of the goals that the disciples in Shakyamuni's order strove to attain.

Prajna Paramita
(The Perfection of Wisdom)

The last of the Six Paramitas is Prajna Paramita. The word "Prajna" means deep wisdom: not just knowledge of this world, but transcendental wisdom that wells up from deep within like an inexhaustible spring. When you attain transcendental wisdom, you can sieve true knowledge from all the knowledge and experiences you have gained in this material world as if you are sieving gold dust from rubble.

To become someone of great stature, you need to have done a great deal of reading and gained a lot of experience. As you continue your efforts, the knowledge and experience you have gained will start to shine like precious gems. Transcendental wisdom shines so brilliantly that it will seem as if worldly knowledge and experiences lose their luster.

The preciousness of transcendental wisdom lies in the fact that you will be able to attain it only when you open the window of your spiritual mind. As you make a constant effort to attain a right state of mind through the practice of the Eightfold Path, your mind will spiritually open, and you will gain the ability to communicate with your own guardian and guiding spirits. Our guardian and guiding spirits in heaven possess far greater wisdom than the wisdom of people living in this world, because spirits in heaven have access to all the knowledge and experiences that they gained from their past incarnations.

While we live in this world on Earth, we only use about 10 percent of our entire consciousness, and the rest remains latent in our subconscious mind. However, when we return to the spirit world, the 90 percent in our subconscious mind becomes our surface consciousness, and the 10 percent in our conscious mind becomes subconscious. So in theory, spirits in heaven should possess nine times as much wisdom as people living on Earth, even if their spiritual awareness was originally at the same level.

In the spirit world, there are many spiritual beings who possess a very high level of awareness. In fact, we can find numerous sages whom we don't have the chance to encounter on Earth. Even the most intelligent scholars and professors in today's world probably do not possess the same level of wisdom as Socrates did, and none of today's philosophers could possibly be a greater thinker than Confucius.

In the spirit world, we can find numerous great figures from recent history, including Socrates and Confucius, as well as divine spirits who played important roles in past civilizations. The wisdom that these spirits use to guide us is at such a high level and of such high quality that it far exceeds the worldly knowledge that we have acquired on Earth. These divine spirits have sent me numerous spiritual messages, and receiving these inspirations from heaven is also part of practicing Prajna Paramita.

It is important to know that the ultimate objective of making an effort in this life is to attain the highest level of wisdom that human beings can reach. Understanding the Truths will help you attain this wisdom, lead you to emancipation, and transform you into a person of immense power.

A Modern Interpretation of the Six Paramitas

Having explained the Six Paramitas, I would like to explore how we can practice them in our daily lives. The Six Paramitas and the Eightfold Path have a lot in common, so in this section, I would like to look at these six disciplines in a new light.

First, I would like to describe Dana Paramita as acts of love. In other words, this is the practice of "love that gives."

The spirit of Sila Paramita, when applied to modern life, can be explained as a revival of stoicism. When you simplify your life and seek intellectual and spiritual values in a plain, stoic lifestyle, you are observing Sila Paramita. Those who make constant efforts to reach high goals feel no need to be pretentious. These people can lead a stoic lifestyle even in modern society and can concentrate their energy on pursuing what is most important to them while remaining unconcerned with minor, worldly matters. This is the stoicism that we can practice in today's society.

Ksanti Paramita is a practice of building inner

strength while waiting patiently until the time is ripe for action. In difficult times, it is important to wait for the right time as we continue to develop our abilities. Instead of trying new things haphazardly, we should wait patiently, as if we are waiting for a jar to be filled up with drips of water. This is the attitude of Ksanti Paramita.

Virya Paramita means making diligent effort. In modern terms, this is equivalent to making an effort to explore and study the teachings of the Truths.

Dhyana Paramita can be understood as the revival of the Eightfold Path. I would like to continue offering explanations of the Eightfold Path in many different ways, because I believe it's important that we set aside time for silence and practice self-reflection based on the Eightfold Path. This practice can be perfected as the path of self-reflection in the Fourfold Path (of love, wisdom, self-reflection, and progress) that I teach at my organization, Happy Science.

Finally, Prajna Paramita corresponds to the second path of the Fourfold Path, which is the path of wisdom. It is my intention to compile all the spiritual wisdom that exists in heaven and to publish it as the books of Truth.

Some of you may have personal experience of spiritual communication with your guardian spirit. As you continue your discipline to clean and polish your mind, you may at some point unlock the door to the spirit world and start receiving inspiration from your guardian spirit.

The five disciplines of giving love, leading a stoic lifestyle, studying with perseverance and diligence, and setting aside time for self-reflection play the important role of protecting those who have opened the window of the spiritual mind from going astray. This is my modern interpretation of the Six Paramitas in today's world.

THE CONCEPT *of* THE VOID

Shakyamuni's Definition of Human Beings

In this chapter, I would like to explore the Buddhist concept of the void. To understand this concept, it is essential to understand the Buddhist view of human beings, life and death, and the world. Without clarifying these points, it is difficult to discuss the idea of void.

The first question I would like to pose is "What does it mean to be human?" Shakyamuni answered this question with a revolutionary definition of human beings. At that time in India, the prevailing belief was that a human being was born with a burden of karma. Indians believed that people's social status was predestined and that their fate was already determined at the time of birth. But Shakyamuni argued that, although the law of karma and other unavoidable factors determine human destiny to a certain extent, we can find a way to overcome and change our destiny when we practice the spiritual disciplines designed to help us attain enlightenment.

This new perspective that Shakyamuni offered was very good news for the people of those times. Many people today may think that Buddhism offers austere teachings and a pessimistic view of the world, but back then, Shakyamuni's teachings were quite revolutionary and offered people hope.

Indian society in Shakyamuni's time was divided into four classes under the rigid caste system: the Brahman, the priest caste; the Kshatriya, the warrior caste; the Vaisya, the merchant caste; and the Sudra, the slave caste. Furthermore, there were people who ranked lower than Sudra; they belonged to the Chandala caste. People in this caste were regarded as disgraceful, were not even considered human, and were treated like cattle. Those who were born into this class remained powerless, without any possibility of improving their lot through their own efforts. Their fate was determined by birth, and there was nothing they could do about it. On the other hand, those born into the Brahman caste were automatically recognized as members of the officiating priest caste, no matter what kind of people they were. Shakyamuni severely questioned this social system.

Shakyamuni thought that Eternal Buddha, the great wisdom that governs the entire universe, would not tolerate a situation like this and that something must be done to overcome the class system. He set out to create a system based on new values. In his order, seekers were given an equal opportunity to practice self-discipline in pursuit of enlightenment, regardless of the class they were born into. Once they became members of Shakyamuni's order, all seekers were given a new status, a new goal, and a new reason to live, regardless of their birth. Shakyamuni thought this system was ideal.

His endeavor was similar to what we are now attempting to achieve at my organization, Happy Science. We are aiming to create a value system based on the Truths. We are undertaking various activities to create a society in which people recognize the value of studying the Truths, and those who are spiritually awakened are held in high regard.

Shakyamuni saw great significance in emancipating those who believed that happiness was out of their reach. That's why he wanted to create new values based on the Truths and bring about a complete change in values set by the rigid, caste-based society. Shakyamuni brought a ray of hope that people could open up a path to true happiness through the practice of self-discipline. And he taught that, to fulfill their hope, they needed first to aspire to become enlightened and then to practice the disciplines.

The Meaning of Life and Death

Next, I would like to look at the Buddhist view of life and death. Back in Shakyamuni's time, India was ravaged by continual wars and attacks by neighboring countries, and people's lives were threatened. The Kapilavastu palace, where Shakyamuni had been brought up, eventually went to rack and ruin. Even Shakyamuni, who was originally the Grand Spirit from the ninth dimension, could not protect his own country and people. All things were indeed impermanent.

In those days, winning battles was basically the only way to survive. To sustain their lives, people had to kill enemies, and only those who were prepared to live even at the cost of others' lives could survive. If they weren't willing to kill their enemies, they had no choice but to die. Being pacifistic or weak meant dying. In this context, it is not surprising that people generally felt that life was futile and yearned strongly for a world after death. They even negated and despised life in this world.

Even among those who sought the path to enlightenment, many longed for happiness in the next life rather than trying to attain Buddhahood in this world. For most of them, life in this world was nothing but suffering, and they wished to return to a world of happiness in the afterlife.

This is why Shakyamuni gave a lot of teachings about life in the next world. He needed to preach faith in the next life because life was so full of misery, suffering, and sadness at that time. Preaching to people about the next life may have been like giving them an anesthetic, but it helped them temporarily free themselves from the anguish and suffering that they could never escape.

The Concept of Reincarnation

Reincarnation is probably the most important idea among the discussions of the meaning of life and death. Other major religions, such as Christianity, Islam, Judaism, Confucianism, and Taoism, do not describe the concept of reincarnation as clearly as Buddhism does. In this sense, the discussion of reincarnations is one of the main characteristics of Buddhism.* Indeed, the fact that Shakyamuni taught this concept explicitly contributed to the spread of his teachings and explains why Buddhist teachings have vast influence in today's world. This influence shows that Buddhism provided teachings of the Truths.

It took great courage for Shakyamuni to publicly introduce such an extraordinary idea as reincarnation. In today's world, people probably do not find the idea of reincarnation far-fetched, because it has become well-known as a teaching of Buddhism. But can you imagine the difficulty of teaching about reincarnation and future and past lives to people who have absolutely no idea about it? Because the idea of reincarnation was connected to the mechanism of the invisible world that nobody could see, hear, or validate, many people found it hard to accept it.

In Shakyamuni's time, people believed in the idea of reincarnation as a form of religious faith. People generally believed in it simply because Shakyamuni said it happened. Not many people were totally convinced that reincarnation was real, but they generally accepted the idea because they respected and trusted Shakyamuni.

The idea of reincarnation was actually not unique to Buddhism. Even the folk religions of India in those days spoke of the transmigration of the soul, but in many cases, they taught that human beings were reincarnated as animals, even lizards and pigeons. The concept that a human soul could transmigrate into all sorts of animals promoted a value for protecting animals and enhanced compassion for life, but it was not a law that could be universally applied. Shakyamuni, who was a very good teacher and storyteller, also spoke of the deer, the pigeon, and other life forms as an expedient way to help people understand the concept of human reincarnation.

In reality, however, human souls have been distinctively human for hundreds of millions of years. There is little possibility of human souls being born in animal bodies. Humans almost always reincarnate as humans, except in very rare cases when human souls temporarily reside in animal bodies for the purpose of special training. Even then, they can only reside in the bodies of highly evolved animals and do so for a short period of a year or two. This special training is arranged to make people feel grateful to be born human. Some human souls reside in domestic animals such as dogs and cats, and because they still possess human senses, living in an animal body is an excruciating experience for them. After they go through this difficult trial, these souls realize how wonderful it is to be human. But as I said earlier, this only occurs rarely, as an exception.

Understanding the idea of reincarnation brings about a revolutionary change in our perspective on life. Most human suffering occurs because people think they only live once. When they become fully aware that this present life is only one point in the eternal flow of time—that they have lived in the past and will live again in the future—they understand that their future lives depend on their present life. This means that they can choose the kind of life they will live in the future.

Consequently, if you wish to live happily in the world after death or in your next incarnation, you need to sow the seeds of happiness now. The efforts you make in this life will lead you to a fulfilling life in the future. The idea of reincarnation guarantees you rewards for the efforts you make now. It is just like accumulating savings that will bring you a large return in years to come. The idea of reincarnation helped guide people in a positive direction, because it encouraged them to make an effort in this lifetime and guaranteed a return in the future.

* Some people argue that Buddhism passively adopted the idea of reincarnation from the folk beliefs of ancient India. One theory interprets Shakyamuni's teaching of egolessness in a materialistic way and denies the existence of the soul and the possibility of reincarnation. Another theory negates the existence of the soul and argues that karma continues to be transmitted from one person to another just as light is passed from one candle to another. However, it is a historical fact that Shakyamuni became an arhat through the attainment of the three types of transcendental wisdom: 1) the ability to know one's own former lives and those of others, 2) the ability to see people's future deaths and births, and 3) the ability to get rid of delusive attachments by realizing Buddhist Truths. These three types of transcendental wisdom can be described as psychic abilities, and they clearly describe the characteristics of Shakyamuni's enlightenment. If there had been no such thing as reincarnation, it would have been impossible for him to penetrate past and future lives. When Shakyamuni taught, he told many stories of past lives and spoke of the possibility of attaining enlightenment in a future life. It is only natural to think that he gained divine powers when he became enlightened. The fact that Shakyamuni possessed the transcendental power to penetrate past and future lives contributed to the evolution of the concept of reincarnation from a folk belief into Truth. In fact, as someone who possesses the same transcendental powers as Shakyamuni had, I cannot help but be surprised at the superficial and worldly interpretations of the truth of reincarnation on the part of Buddhist scholars long after Shakyamuni's passing.

The Discovery of the Spirit World

So far, I have discussed the Buddhist views of human existence, life and death, and reincarnation. I would now like to tell you how Shakyamuni recognized the other world—the spirit world.

After Shakyamuni's order grew to be an organization with several thousand followers, he began to give sermons once a week to a congregation. For the rest of the week, he limited his activities to a few meetings with leading disciples. In this way, he secured ample time for meditation. While meditating outdoors, his mind would often leave his body and travel to the spirit world.

Shakyamuni's understanding of the spirit world was quite advanced at that time. He already understood the nature of the ninth-dimensional Cosmic Realm. He was aware that the world of the ninth dimension existed only in Earth's spirit world but also extended to the realms surrounding other planets. He knew that highly advanced spirits existed on other planets and that they too were undergoing spiritual discipline to improve themselves.

When he experienced the infinite expansion of his spiritual self becoming one with the grand universe, he felt this planet Earth shrink to a tiny dot, as small as one of the cells in an internal organ. Through this experience, he came to understand how it felt to be the universe itself, but it was extremely difficult to explain such enlightenment to his disciples. At that time in India, people did not have a high enough level of awareness to understand the structure of the universe, so Shakyamuni was only able to teach this idea using metaphors.

I have been revealing the truths about the multidimensional structure of the spirit world. And Shakyamuni possessed the same knowledge more than 2,500 years ago, although his understanding was limited to the framework of thought that prevailed in ancient India. If I were to point out anything missing in Shakyamuni's understanding, it would be this: in his astral travel to the other world, he was only able to contact those who resided in the Indian realm of the spirit world, because his view of the world did not extend beyond India. It was very difficult for him to contact those inhabiting other areas of the spirit world. He did see many spirits who took on various lifestyles that seemed peculiar to him, but he did not go as far as exploring where they belonged or what kind of lives they led. However, his astral travels gave him experiences of the spirit world that helped him greatly when he taught the meaning of life and death, the purpose of human life, and reincarnation. His discovery of the spirit world added height, depth, and authenticity to his thoughts.

Shakyamuni's experience of the spirit world was similar to my own, in that I received messages from a variety of spirits from heaven, which I published as books of spiritual messages. I believe that the publication of these books helped people accept and believe in the existence of the divine spirits in heaven. These books also laid the foundations for the publication of my teachings of the Truths.

Religion is the science of the spirit world. Any teaching that is not grounded in knowledge of the spirit world is philosophy. It would not be an exaggeration to say that the difference between philosophy and religion is the commitment on the part of religion to explore the spirit world in a scientific manner.

A New Perspective on the Physical World

When you become aware of the existence of the spirit world, how will this three-dimensional, physical world look? Visiting the spirit world can be likened to traveling abroad. It is like going to a foreign country for the first time in your life and experiencing a life and culture that are completely different from your own. If you have had a one-year stay in a place in an abundant natural environment, for instance, on returning home to a crowded city, all the familiar places packed with people and the narrow streets congested with traffic may seem foreign to you.

Similarly, once you have seen the spirit world, the way people live in this physical world will seem odd. This strangeness stems partly from a difference in values. From the perspective of heaven, the way people live in this world, busily working away day after day, makes them look like ants carrying granules of sugar. Just as we humans feel pity for ants toiling at the task of collecting food, which they probably believe is the supreme objective of their lives, when you know the values of the spirit world, you will feel that people in the material world are making vain attempts to attain something of small value.

But this is only the first step you take when looking at this world from a spiritual perspective. The next step is to ask why such a transient and futile world should exist. As you contemplate this question deeply and try to understand the true meaning of this physical world, you will realize that, although the things of this world seem ephemeral, they have all been provided for us as important materials we can use to learn and progress in our spiritual discipline. Furthermore, you will become aware that the physical body and the spirit body are basically made of the same elements, and this is also true of the materials of this world and those of the spirit world; they all simply manifest themselves differently.

Souls are essentially created by the Light of Eternal Buddha (God), and everything in the physical world is a manifestation of His energy. We manifest ourselves differently just as water vapor turns into water when it's cooled and ice when it's frozen. Water vapor is like the soul, and ice is like the physical body. They may look different, but they are the same substance manifesting differently.

When your awareness of the world deepens, you will understand that both this world and the other are essentially the same. When you reach this level of understanding, your perceptions of this physical world will make a complete turnaround from negative to positive. You will start to see Eternal Buddha's grand plan and purpose behind the creation of this material world.

The Buddhist Interpretation of the Void

The theme of the last section, "a new perspective on the physical world," is actually related to the Buddhist idea of void. You have probably heard the phrase "matter is void—void is matter" in the Heart Sutra. This is considered one of the most important Buddhist teachings, and knowing this phrase seems to be the key to understanding Buddhism.

There are two levels of understanding the idea of void. The first level is to distinguish this world from the other world. In the phrase "matter is void," "matter" refers to the physical world. So the phrase means that this physical world is transient and temporary; everything in this world will eventually perish. Each and every person, whether of humble or noble birth, will eventually die. Their bodies will perish, and only the soul will return to the other world. "Matter" may be visible to our eyes, but it exists only temporarily. It will change its form and eventually disappear from this world when it enters the other world. The other world, or the spirit world, is described as "void" because it's invisible to our eyes.

The phrase "void is matter" means that souls incarnate into this world for the purpose of spiritual discipline. They go through the cycle of reincarnation over and over again to experience life in a physical body. The phrase "void is matter" describes how the invisible existence transforms into the visible existence when the soul is born into a physical body. So the first step in understanding the idea of void is to know the difference between this world and the other world, and to understand the cycle of reincarnation between these two worlds.

The next step is related to the question "What is the essential nature of the element that constitutes both this world and the other?" To answer this question, I would like to introduce a philosophy that states that all existence is composed of the Light of Eternal Buddha (God). The world has a multilayered structure, ranging from the third to the ninth dimension, but everything is essentially a manifestation of the Light. Only the Light is true existence; it transforms itself to create the various states of the world, both material and spiritual. Both the spirit body and the light body (enveloped within the spirit body) are made of the Light. To manifest itself in this three-dimensional, material world, the Light first takes the form of the basic particles called "spiritons," which become the elementary particles that constitute physical materials.

This perspective on the world is in line with leading-edge modern physics, which has discovered that elementary particles have the attributes of both particles and waves. This makes sense when we consider the truth that everything in this world, both material and spiritual, is a manifestation of the Light.

All materials in this world are made of the spiritual energy of the Light, and material existence changes its form and resolves into spiritual energy. This concept of the circulation of energy and matter explains the phrase "matter is void—void is matter." Advances in modern science have made it possible to explain the idea of void in the context of physics.

The Significance of the Void

My previous discussion of the concept of void leads to the following questions: "Why is the idea of void so important?" "Why did Shakyamuni Buddha teach the idea of void?" "Why is it necessary to talk about the invisible world?'" and "Why should the invisible turn into the visible and the visible into the invisible?" In this section, I would like to attempt to answer these questions.

Asking these questions in fact led to the rise of Zen Buddhism. Zen Buddhists practice what they call the Zen dialogue, which is a series of seemingly nonsensical questions and answers. The purpose of Zen dialogue is to awaken seekers to their divine nature and the truth of the spirit world. The idea behind this practice is that, as you contemplate a theme that seems totally unrelated to yourself, your true thoughts and circumstances become visible, as if they are reflected in a mirror. In this sense, we can say that the idea of the void gave rise to the emergence of Zen Buddhism, although the current Zen philosophy has veered from the original teachings of Shakyamuni.

People become attached to the things of this world when they believe this world to be real existence. They become attached to their physical bodies, romantic relationships, or food. However, these attachments will not bring peace of mind. It is only when we let go of our attachments that we enjoy serenity within, which brings us a sense of true happiness. Shakyamuni taught the idea of void because he was fully aware of this truth.

Shakyamuni taught his disciples, "Listen people, you may believe that the visible things of this world—your physical body, material objects, and all living things in nature—are real and substantial, but they are all temporary. Their real existence is only 'void.' All matter is void." Can you imagine the magnitude of the shock his disciples experienced?

But if you have ever looked at an object through an electron microscope, you understand the truth of the phrase, "matter is void." When magnified, what seems to be a solid object becomes an aggregate of particles with a lot of space between them. Although the material things of this world seem real, they are optical illusions.

Shakyamuni taught the idea of void because he wanted to liberate people's minds, which were attached to the material things of this world, and awaken people to the true values of the other world. This first stage of denial is related to the origin of Zen. However, the idea of "matter is void" did not convey the whole truth, so he taught the other side of the truth, which is "void is matter."

To explain this idea, Shakyamuni taught that the Will of Eternal Buddha (God) created all things in this world. Although we could neither see nor touch His Will, everything in this world manifested when His Will became His words. This planet called Earth, and all the animals and plants on it, came into being through the Will of Eternal Buddha. This world was created by His Will and by the work of divine spirits who devoted themselves to disseminating His Will. The teaching that "matter is void and void is matter" clearly shows how well-balanced Shakyamuni's thought was.

To conclude, Shakyamuni taught the idea of void as a spiritual discipline for getting rid of worldly attachments. He also taught people about the origin of this world and human life and revealed the secrets of Creation. These are the reasons the idea of void has been considered a very important teaching.

The Transience of All Things

I would like to discuss another Buddhist teaching in relation to the idea of void, which is the idea that all things are transient. This phrase appears at the beginning of *The Tale of the Heike*, a famous war chronicle of the Heike clan, written in the thirteenth-century Japan. This phrase has a sad tone, with the pathos of the vanquished and the dying. The author of *The Tale of the Heike* probably wanted to express how he saw the transience of human life in the rise and fall of powerful clans.

But Shakyamuni's idea of the transience of all things was based on his steadfast awareness of the existence of the spirit world. The phrase "all things are transient" does not only describe the ever-changing nature of existence from the perspective of this world. It also describes the ever-changing vicissitudes of human life from the perspective of the other world.

Only those who have fully grasped the unchanging nature within this ever-changing world can understand the true meaning of this world. All human deeds will eventually be washed away and disappear in the passage of time. Only those who can see what is unchanging and eternal in the flow of a river that carries away all human endeavor can understand the futility of the passing of this world in its truest sense.

The idea of the transience of all things was never intended to be a pessimistic view of life. It described the state of this world from the perspective of the spirit world. This idea can be applied to today's world as well. When you truly awaken to the world of the Truths, you may feel the emptiness of the business world. You may find nothing of value in the volumes of literature you have read. When you face the vast ocean of the Truths, you will feel that all the things of this world are like bubbles in the sea that are bound to disappear. To understand the true meaning of life in this world, it is necessary to continue learning what is of true spiritual value and to absorb what nourishes the soul.

To conclude this discussion of the phrase "all things are transient," I would like to say that this idea should not be understood simply as a pessimistic view of life. This phrase describes how the value and importance that we usually place on this world fade when we see this world from the perspective of the other world. Days spent competing for promotions or pursuing love affairs will seem worthless. But still, understanding this is only the first step toward enlightenment.

A Comparison of Void and Nothingness

There is another concept very similar to the idea of void, which is the idea of nothingness. This is a vast subject in itself, and it would perhaps require a book to discuss it in detail, so in this section I would like to give a brief explanation of this idea.

The ideas of void and nothingness sound similar, but they don't mean the same thing. As I have explained, void does not mean that nothing exists; rather, it describes the ever-changing state of Eternal Buddha's (God's) energy, which transforms into a multiplicity of forms. Void is the process by which physical existence turns into spiritual existence and vice versa. The idea of void encapsulates the law of constant change and cycle of motion in the universe: birth, growth, decline, and death.

On the other hand, nothingness does not express the cycle of motion in the universe. It is simply a negation of existence. From this standpoint, we can say that void is a concept of time and nothingness is a concept of existence.

The key to unlocking the secrets of void is the notion of time. This idea expresses the essential nature of time. The concept of time involves change, and time cannot exist in a space where there is no change, where everything has stopped and remains completely still. Time is generated only when all things constantly change and transform themselves—when they are mutable. So the idea of void is actually a theory of time. Time infers the recurring process of birth, growth, decline, and death.

On the other hand, the idea of nothingness can be explained as the theory of existence. What, then, is the nature of nothingness in relation to the theory of existence? To answer this question, we need to understand this idea in relation to the Will of the Creator of this universe.

We think of existence as something solid, unchanging, and stable. But the idea of nothingness is like a Zen koan, which asks us whether this way of seeing the world is in fact right. It poses questions such as "Does the house you live in really exist?" "Does the Earth really exist?" "Do you really exist?" "How about the land you stand on, the rocks, and the animals?" In other words, the idea of nothingness confronts us with the question, "If time stops, is it possible for things to exist?"

While the idea of void involves the passage of time, time is halted in the idea of nothingness; nothingness asks us whether this world or the entire universe can exist if time is frozen into a single moment. When you contemplate this, you will realize that this physical world that we believe to be real is actually nothing more than a projection of the Will of Eternal Buddha (God), the origin of all existence. This means that the multilayered structure of the world, which consists of the ninth, eighth, seventh, sixth, fifth, fourth, and third dimensions, is also nothing more than the projection of His Will. They are simply images reflected on a screen, just like the images of landscapes and people that we see on a movie screen. If you were to look at this screen of the spirit world, you'd see tathagatas of the eighth dimension, bodhisattvas of the seventh dimension, the inhabitants of the sixth dimension, and maybe even evil spirits from hell at the bottom of the fourth dimension. But they would only be images projected onto a screen, so as soon as the light projector was shut off, the images would disappear. This is the truth of existence. The idea of nothingness explains that the world is the projection of Eternal Buddha's Will and that, as such, all existence can suddenly come into being or disappear, according to His Will.

The ideas of the void and nothingness may sound very similar, but the first is a theory of time, and the second is a theory of space. Both ideas represent perspectives on the world: a perspective on time (void) and a perspective on space or existence (nothingness).

A New Development of the Void

The concept of void will eventually merge with leading-edge ideas in physics. At present, the field of physics seems not to have made much progress in understanding elementary particles and the structure of the universe. But beyond the boundaries of today's understanding, the mystical wonders of the spirit world await modern physics. A breakthrough in physics will require the unraveling of the secrets of the mechanism and structure of the spirit world.

A modern or futuristic interpretation of the void leads us to the analysis of Divine Light as the source of elementary particles. This is the science of the spirit world, which goes beyond Einstein's theory of relativity. Einstein's theory states that warps occur in time and space, based on the assumption that the velocity of light is constant. While Newtonian physics explained laws based on the premise that time and space are constant, Einstein's theory was based on the idea that light has a constant velocity. Based on this theory, Einstein discovered that time and space can be distorted: time can be lengthened and shortened, and space can be warped.

But Einstein's theory will be overturned when spiritual velocity is discovered. This discovery will override the centrality of the velocity of light. It will show that the velocity of light cannot be the ultimate criterion, because it is not constant. Spiritual velocity is faster than the speed of light, which is why spirits in the other world can see the future. If we can travel faster than light, we can see light before the sun emits sunlight. In other words, it is possible to see the world of tomorrow. I would like to conclude this chapter with the prediction that spiritual velocity will be the basis of the physics of tomorrow.

THE LAW *of* CAUSALITY

The Concept of Spiritual Bonds

In this chapter, I would like to focus on the law of causality, which is another important key to understanding Shakyamuni Buddha's teachings. In Japan, where there is a long tradition of Buddhism, many people still believe that an invisible tie exists between people, and they greatly value this idea. For example, they use an expression, "Even the person whose shoulder you accidentally brush against has some connection to you from past lives."

In fact, the idea of love is behind this way of looking at human relationships: people as interconnected by invisible bonds. From this perspective, even someone that seems to come into your life by chance has a spiritual bond with you and was in fact preordained to meet you. This may sound like a fatalistic idea, but it is actually a positive thing, instead of distancing yourself from others, to acknowledge that divine guidance has created a spiritual connection between you and other people.

I estimate that the current population of the spirit

world is more than fifty billion. Of these, only a limited number of souls are born into a particular place in a particular era. These souls develop relationships with one another through the process of creating a civilization or culture in that specific region or nation. This means that the people you encounter are part of the very specific group of souls that you belong to, and that in their past lives, many of them were born into the same era and the same place as you were. In fact, if you could see the past lives of people around you, you would find that you have had relationships with most of them in your past lives.

Of the numerous people you encounter in this world, you probably develop particularly close relationships with certain people, such as your friends, your spouse, your teachers, or your students. In most cases, we do not build these relationships by coincidence. We most likely had close relationships with such people in past lives, too. In the cycle of reincarnation, we often build special relationships—parents and children, brothers and sisters, friends and colleagues—within the same group of people. Of course, we also develop new relationships and create new spiritual ties in this life, but even these are often guided by heaven. These spiritual bonds develop into new relationships in our future.

Human relationship is a chain of invisible bonds, and your successes and failures in life have a lot to do with how you relate to others. Your business may succeed or fail, and you may get promoted or demoted, depending on what kinds of relationships you form with the people around you. The Buddhist concept of the spiritual bond that exists among people is actually a theory of human relationships; it is a new perspective on the philosophy of love.

The Law of Cause and Effect

Following my brief discussion of the spiritual bonds among people, I would like to talk about the law of cause and effect, which is also a distinctive Buddhist teaching. Based on the idea of spiritual bonds, we can say, for example, that the reason you got married to your partner was because you had a close relationship with him or her in a past life. This idea, when developed into a more general theory, can be explained as the law of cause and effect, in which certain actions bring about certain results. This law states that a good cause will bring about a good effect and a bad cause will bring about a bad effect. The law of cause and effect is one of the most fundamental laws that govern human life. The success of Buddhism both as a philosophy and as a religion lies in the fact that it has a deep insight into this law of cause and effect.

Why do we keep building relationships with the same group of people? It is because, whether they were our parents, children, brothers, sisters, or spouse, we have enjoyed relationships with those we are now close to in our past lives. Because we were happy to be with them in the past, we chose to form relationships with the same people again in this lifetime.

Every day, we are sowing the seeds for our future. The seeds of causes we plant today will sprout, grow, and come back to us as results in the future. The law of cause and effect is actually the Buddhist philosophy of success as well as the philosophy of happiness. People often misunderstand Buddhism as a philosophy that teaches human suffering and focuses on the negative aspects of life, but this is wrong. Like many other great philosophers, Shakyamuni taught the philosophy of happiness, which essentially can be summarized by the phrase "the law of cause and effect."

If we want to harvest the fruit of happiness, we need to sow the seeds of happiness, water them, fertilize them, and expose them to the sun to help them grow. This is actually a rule of achieving success that we can apply to every aspect of our daily lives.

Of course, the effort we make may sometimes not be rewarded directly. For example, you may fail a college entrance exam even though you studied extremely hard. However, your hard work will never be wasted; it will bring about a positive effect on your future. On the other hand, as the proverb says, "Bad news travels fast": if you engage in malicious activities behind people's back, they will come to be known sooner or later and will eventually bring you misfortune.

If you see life as a dynamic activity based on specific rules, you can see it as the manifestation of a chain of cause and effect. Whether the seeds you have sown will bear fruit in this lifetime is uncertain, but what is certain is that you will never be able to harvest fruits unless you have first sown the seeds.

Shakyamuni taught that we should continually sow seeds of happiness for the future instead of simply lamenting any unhappiness that has resulted from our past deeds. This was the reason he taught the importance of making diligent efforts, giving offerings to others, and conveying the Truths to guide others to the right path. These virtuous acts will bring us happiness in the end. We may not be able to reap the harvest of our efforts during this lifetime, but the time will come when we receive the fruits after we return to heaven. We are storing up treasure in our storehouse in heaven as we do good deeds in this world. I hope you have understood that the law of cause and effect is a theory of attaining happiness within the flow of time.

What Is Karma?

This discussion of the law of cause and effect leads us to consider the idea of karma. You have probably heard of the idea that human beings have good or bad karma. Everyone is supposed to be born equal, but everyone is different, not only in outward appearance, but also in the inner life. Where do these differences originate? The reason for these differences is not necessarily found in present life; the cumulative effects of our past lives in the eternal cycle of reincarnation also influence our current state.

When we look at karma as a rule, it can be either good or bad, but people tend to associate the word "karma" with a negative connotation. In the Buddhist tradition, too, the concept of karma was often used to explain the reason for people's misfortunes in the present life. Buddhists believed that, for example, someone hurt you in this life because you hurt someone else in a past life; you are blind in this life because you damaged someone's sight in a past life; you have a disabled leg because you injured someone else's legs in a past life;

you are humiliated in this life because you humiliated someone in a past life; you are cursed now because you cursed someone in a past life, and so on. According to this logic, the accumulation of past wrongdoings results in karma, which has a negative influence on your present life. Many people understand karma as the idea that your unhappiness or failure in this life is caused by the resentment, grudges, and other negative thoughts that you provoked in a past life.

Based on the past-life readings I have conducted, I can say that events from past lives do have some bearing on present life. Life is like a workbook of problems to solve, and from this perspective, the most distinctive problems that we face result from our actions not only in this life, but also in past lives. But this does not necessarily mean that the difficulties we face in life are simply punishment for the wrongdoings we committed in past lives.

It is certainly possible for someone who committed a murder in a past life to be murdered in this life. But this does not necessarily occur as punishment for his past crime. He may have chosen to take the role of victim in this life, because we often learn through experience. Some people choose a difficult life so that they can learn by going through the same harm they inflicted on others in their past lives.

Our life plan is not supposed to be filled with only good things. Our life is planned so that we take all the necessary steps to grow and develop our soul to the highest level possible. We knew we would face these difficulties, because each of us drew up a life plan before we came down to this world.

Karma is the imprint of memories from past lives that remains in each soul, and so karma can be understood as the tendencies of the soul. Everyone's soul has unique characteristics, and when we face situations similar to those we have faced in past lives, we tend to repeat the same patterns of action and get caught in the same sorts of traps over and over again. To find the tendencies of your soul, you can ask yourself, "What are the most unique aspects of my soul? What sorts of problems am I likely to encounter in my life?" The answers to these questions will vary from person to person.

I would like you to understand the word "karma" as the tendencies of the soul. When you become aware of your own tendencies and carefully consider how to handle the issues you face, you can start living a constructive life.

The Idea of Fatalism

The discussions of the law of cause and effect and of karma may have left some of you wondering where fatalism fits in, so let us now consider the subject of fate. We can start by examining whether karma and destiny mean the same thing. In fact, karma is one of the elements that constitute destiny.

Let me explain this using an analogy. Each car has its own distinctive characteristics. Some are fast, while others are more fuel efficient. Some are made for cities, while others are made for suburbs. Some are low-powered, while others are made to carry a heavy load. The tendencies of our souls are like the different characteristics of cars.

Imagine that navigating your life is just like driving a car. You have to drive in the way that best suits the characteristics of the car. Destiny is like the course of your life, and karma is like the type of the vehicle you are driving to travel through the road of destiny. Karma can also be likened to the type of boat you take to go down the river of destiny.

You can foresee the outcome of your life to a certain degree when you assess the tendencies of your soul in any given circumstance. You can do this in a similar way to how you bowl. If you release the ball in a certain direction with a certain amount of force, you can estimate how many pins you will be able to knock down. This is how you can predict the outcome of your life.

So is our life determined by fate? There are a number of factors that make up our destiny; however, what they consist of and how much influence they will have on our life depends on each person. The first factor is karma, or the tendencies of the soul; the second is the family environment in which you are brought up; the third factor is the social environment and the times in which you live; the fourth is the effort you make; and the fifth is the assistance of others.

Of these five factors that form your destiny, we can still change the fourth and the fifth factors—your efforts and others' support. Other factors—the tendencies of your soul and the circumstances you were born into—have been pretty much fixed. So while our life is predestined to a certain degree, we can also change our life through the efforts we make and help we receive from others.

To conclude this section, I would like to say that our destiny is created based on the combination of predetermined conditions and other changeable factors.

5 The Nature of Free Will

In connection to the discussion of destiny, I would now like to turn to the topic of free will. If I were asked whether we have free will, I would say yes. But our free will is also restricted by external factors to a certain extent.

Let me illustrate how our free will works using an example. Let's say you got on the last car of a packed train at rush hour, and you want to move all the way through to the front car. It is almost impossible to elbow your way through before you get to your destination. In theory, you could walk all the way from the last car to the first car, but it is practically impossible because of all the passengers blocking your way. But you could easily do this during off-peak hours. This analogy shows the key to understanding the working of free will.

During the course of your life, there are times when you are hampered by external factors and other times when you can move forward by your own will. We need to determine which of these situations you are facing. If you find that you cannot open a path by your own effort, just as when you are blocked in a packed train, then you need to find an alternative route. One way is to wait for the right time. Other passengers will eventually get off the train and make room for you to move forward. Another way is to get off the train, walk along the platform toward the front, and get on the train again. The latter case ignores the premise that, metaphorically, you are on the train and can't really get off, but it suggests that you need to find an unconventional method to exercise your free will. There are moments in life when something totally unexpected happens and completely changes the course of your life, as if you are born anew. So when you cannot use ordinary methods to move forward, it is possible to find a new way.

Thus, there are basically two levels of free will. The first level is free will within an ordinary context. In this case, you have to simply wait for the situation to change. The second level is to exercise your free will in an exceptional way. This is equivalent to having the courage to get off the train, move forward on the platform, and get on the train again.

Attaining enlightenment through spiritual training in Buddhism corresponds with getting off the train when you cannot move ahead in a packed train. You have to do this at the risk of not getting on the train again before the doors shut. Perhaps this risk can be likened to the hardship that accompanies self-discipline on the path to enlightenment. In essence, the discipline for attaining enlightenment opens a new path to the future and lets you achieve unexpected results.

The Concept of Hell

Further exploration on the law of causality will lead us to contemplate the concepts of heaven and hell. In contrast to Christianity, Buddhism gives detailed and elaborate descriptions of heaven and hell. This is because Shakyamuni himself, while living on Earth, traveled to many different realms in the other world.

During meditation, Shakyamuni would often slip out of his body and visit different realms of heaven and hell. Upon his return, he would share with his disciples detailed accounts of what he saw. As Shakyamuni kept telling stories of the other world, his disciples gradually formed a clearer picture of heaven and hell and deepened their belief in the world of the afterlife.

While Buddhism offers clear descriptions of the realms of hell, Christianity simply teaches that those who do not believe in Christ will go to hell, so it is hard to learn specific details about hell from Christian teachings. We can find the descriptions of various realms of hell and the appearances of the inhabitants of hell in Buddhist teachings, because Shakyamuni himself possessed advanced spiritual powers. Another reason is that many of his disciples, including those who lived in later years, possessed psychic abilities that enabled them to grasp what kind of world hell was.

There were two main objectives for teaching about hell. The first objective was to educate people. Those who believed that death was the end of their life were easily tempted by worldly pleasures and suffered from attachments to the physical world. But Buddhism taught that life continues on even after the physical death and that those who had vicious thoughts and deeds during their lifetime on Earth would unquestionably be subject to severe judgment in the afterlife. This teaching aroused people's fears and at the same time helped them strengthen their faith.

No matter what era they are born into, advanced souls are capable of learning advanced teachings. But it is hard for developing souls to believe or learn the Truths unless they become aware of the possibility of being struck by a disaster or misfortune. Teaching about hell was an expedient to awakening and saving people's souls.

The second objective for teaching about hell was to clarify the true nature of human existence. After we leave this material world, our thoughts become who we are. If our minds are filled with diabolical thoughts, we will take on the appearance of a devil. Those whose minds are full of vengeful thoughts will turn into vengeful ghosts. The world of hell is proof that human thoughts can become real and that evil thoughts can cause a vile reality.

The Reality of Hell

Many people probably think that hell is just an imaginary place, but hell is a reality. This does not mean that Eternal Buddha (God) created hell. But for those who dwell there, hell is as real as it gets.

What sorts of dreams do you have when you are sick with a high fever? Perhaps they are dreams about a dark, cold, and deserted place. You may have had dreams of someone chasing you to kill you or of falling into a hole or getting in a bad accident. In our bad dreams, we get a glimpse of the world of hell. Hell is a place where your nightmare becomes the reality.

The good thing about a nightmare is that it ends when you wake up. But the nightmare of hell could last hundreds of years. The inhabitants of hell keep saying, "I must be having a bad dream. Something this absurd cannot be real." But, oddly enough, this nightmare does not end, and it seems real. They cannot get out of the world of hell until they change their minds.

Heaven and hell do not exist somewhere in the invisible world. Heaven does not exist up in the sky, nor hell underneath the ground. Heaven and hell exist in the same world we live in. The other world coexists with this world, because our inner worlds are connected to the invisible world.

Although hell and heaven are invisible to human eyes, they exist in the same space as the world we live in. They exist on the streets we walk, in the buildings we work in, and in the schools where we study. Spirits of hell might be killing each other on the same paved street where you are walking now. This may sound strange, but your thoughts or your mind could become the reality. You can think of the other world as a place where your dreams become the reality and your reality becomes dreams.

You may have had dreams that seemed very real, or you may have recaptured the thread of the same dream you have had before. These dreams could be a continuation of the experiences you had during your previous visit to the spirit world. You could be visiting the spirit world again and seeing these experiences as your dreams.

So if you would like to know whether your mind is in tune with heaven or hell, try examining your dreams. If you often dream of sharing joy with others in a peaceful place, then your mind is attuned to heaven. If, on the other hand, you often have dreams of experiencing difficult situations, feeling depressed and sad, or having no peace of mind, then it means that you are visiting hell in your sleep. Our dreams can tell us what kind of world we are going to return to after we die.

What will you do when the dream is no longer a dream but a reality? The only thing you can rely on at that time is your understanding of the Truths. This will be the key that determines your destination in the afterworld. You will know how to escape from the nightmare of hell if you've learned and understood the Truths while you are alive. Those who have not studied the Truths will have absolutely no idea what to do. There is no school in hell where you can learn how to escape from the agony of hell. The saying, "Knowledge is power" holds true in the world of the afterlife.

The Concept of Heaven

Following our exploration of hell, let us look at the Buddhist concept of heaven. Buddhism divides heaven into roughly three realms. First, there is the realm of human beings; this is a world where good-natured people go. Second, there is the realm of heaven, and this is a world where those who were able to polish their mind through spiritual discipline return. Above these two realms exists the realm of Buddhahood, and this world is inhabited by deities. This is the Buddhist description of heaven.

From my observation, however, the world of heaven is divided into many more levels, and the inhabitants of each realm have different attributes. Heaven has a very intricate structure composed of carefully segmented realms. Although I often describe heaven using the terms fourth, fifth, sixth, seventh, eighth, and ninth dimensions, each dimension is actually subdivided into smaller worlds. This is because the other world is a world of consciousness or thoughts, so even a slight difference in the level of their awareness causes the spirits to live in separate worlds.

Heaven is roughly divided into the following levels: the World of Goodness (fifth dimension), where the inhabitants have a natural disposition toward goodness; the World of Light (sixth dimension), where the inhabitants have contributed to society through their success while at the same time possessing an inner quality of goodness; and, above these, the World of Bodhisattvas (the seventh dimension) and the World of Tathagatas (the eighth dimension), where the highly evolved divine spirits or angels live.

Buddhism acknowledges the existence of heavenly spirits and recognizes that a variety of spirits live in heaven. One of the distinctive characteristics of Buddhism is that it describes divine spirits engaged in different types of work. The other world is simply an extension of this world. All of us living in this world will eventually return to the other world, so the spirit world cannot be completely different from the world we live in now. Just as people living in this world have work to do, the inhabitants of the other world have tasks they fulfill.

The Reality of Heaven

What is heaven really like? How would you feel if you were actually there? Heaven is often described as a place filled with brilliant light. Some call it the world of perpetual bliss or of everlasting summer. Others call it the world of joy. If I were to describe heaven using the terms of this world, I would say that heaven is a place where close friends get together and enjoy talking with one another.

The most distinctive characteristic of the inhabitants of heaven is, in a word, innocence. Their hearts are artless and pure. They have hearts of gold, which is the basic requirement for living in heaven. The inhabitants of heaven are always kind to others and at the same time willing to do what is truly good for themselves. They are filled with a wish to spread happiness around them without causing harm to others.

If I were to describe the requirement for living in heaven in simple terms, it would be to always live with a smile on your face. The smile on your face should not be a superficial one, but a natural one that comes from your heart. This is the requirement for living in heaven. If you look back on yourself and cannot tell where you went wrong, try this simple mental exercise: imagine that you've lost social status, position, or reputation, and examine honestly whether you would still be able to live with a natural smile on your face.

Another guideline for entering the world of heaven is to check whether many people have disliked you during your life. This may sound too simple, but in heaven, you will only find people who are liked by others. The reason these people are liked by others is that they liked others. This is a rule that applies to everyone. So, if you wish to return to heaven, you have to be someone who is sincere, who always has a smile on your face, who gives love to many, and who is liked by many. Fulfilling these simple requirements is the key to opening the door of heaven.

If you ever feel proud of your shrewdness but often find yourself disliked by many, stop for a moment and think. What kind of world would this kind of person return to? Being liked by others does not mean craving love from others. What I am trying to say is that those whose presence makes others uncomfortable cannot live in heaven. Heaven is a place where all your thoughts become transparent and others can see into your mind. You cannot live in harmony with others if you have evil thoughts in your mind. A flock of sheep will not be able to graze peacefully if there is a wolf among them. So one way to describe heaven is that it is a place inhabited by those who feel comfortable showing what they think. In contrast, people whose minds are unclean and filled with vile, evil, or filthy thoughts will not be allowed to live in heaven.

Would you feel comfortable if you were to expose all your thoughts to others? If you feel the need to hide certain thoughts or feelings, then it may take a while for you to return to heaven.

An ideal way of life for human beings is a life that both you and others can appreciate, a life in which you are honest, innocent, and true to yourself. Living in heaven is as simple as that.

It is essential to first live the kind of life that both you and others can celebrate. Then, as the next step, you can take on more important tasks as an angel to influence a greater number of people.

The Creation of an Ideal World on Earth

In this chapter, I have explored the topics of fatalism, free will, and heaven and hell from the perspective of the law of causality. Buddhism taught the concept of heaven and hell to show that the seeds we sow every day create heaven or hell. It taught the importance of leading a heavenly life while still living in this world to achieve the goal of creating "Buddhaland," or a utopian world on Earth where all people live together in harmony and fulfillment.

What kinds of seeds do we need to sow to achieve this goal? First, we must gain a deep understanding of the law of causality, and then we must live in a way that will not bring harm to others or ourselves. We must live in a way that will increase the happiness of ourselves, as well as others.

Some may say that good people lose out in the end and that honesty doesn't pay. But I say that we should do good and we should be honest. Artless, trusting, honest people may seem naive, but their way of life contributes to the creation of an ideal world on Earth.

We should live with a sincere and honest heart. Never try to bring harm to others. Believe that everything is in the process of purification and progress. In other words, we should live in the way that angels would live on Earth.

Creating a utopian world on Earth is not an easy task, but it can be achieved when each and every person understands the law of causality. Life consists of chains of cause and effect, so as long as you keep an attitude of sowing good causes, you will be surrounded by good results in time.

Difficult circumstances and unfavorable situations are merely the fruits of seeds you have sown in the past. What you should do now, at this moment, is concentrate on sowing good seeds for the future. This is the very essence of the philosophy of positive thinking, and this way of thinking allows you to live a life filled with light. To practice positive thinking, you need a deep understanding of the law of causality. The difficult situation you are facing now may be the harvest of tares you sowed earlier, but as long as you concentrate on sowing good seeds from this point on, you can expect a good harvest in the future. If you continue to live with this philosophy in your mind, you will see the world around you turning into a world filled with golden light. I hope that many people start living in this way.

SIX

THE PHILOSOPHY *of* HUMAN PERFECTION

What Is Enlightenment?

In this final chapter, I would like to explore enlightenment, which is both a classic and a new theme. Shakyamuni's teaching of enlightenment for individuals remains a source of fascination to many. What is unique about the concept of enlightenment is that it depicts humans as strong beings that are firmly standing with both feet on the ground and are aiming to grow boldly, instead of helpless beings waiting to be saved by an outside power. This must be one of the secrets of Buddhism's popularity.

At the root of Buddhist teachings lies a belief in the strength of human beings. Some may see Buddhism as a pessimistic and weak religion, but Buddhism actually offers methods for becoming a strong and independent self. In Shakyamuni's time, 2,500 years ago, his teaching that each and every individual could attain enlightenment and become a Buddha, or an awakened one, was truly an epoch-making idea. Contrary to what some believe, this idea was not developed by the Mahayana schools in later years. Its source can be traced back to the time when Shakyamuni delivered his first sermon to the five seekers, whom he acknowledged had attained the enlightenment of arhats.

We human beings can live for the sake of others, for society, or for our country, but we each begin our life from the self and come back to the self at the end of our life. That's why any ideology or theory that neglects the individual self often does not bear fruit in the end. For example, communism advocates that the highest good is to work for the sake of the state, but this idea eventually leads people to lose their motivation to work and their desire to improve themselves.

The idea of enlightenment leads us to a discussion of how we perceive the individual in relation to the whole. Originally, each soul was a part of the whole; individual souls were originally part of the life form of Eternal Buddha (God). The reason we split off and became individual souls is that each one of us is expected to develop our own character and shine our unique light.

Of course, we should aim to improve the whole of humanity, but the journey to that ultimate goal starts with our individual efforts to refine our own character. We cannot simply lump people together and treat them as a mass, with no difference from one another. The Light split apart to create individual souls, each with unique characteristics of its own, so it is important that each of us shines with our own unique brilliance.

Enlightenment certainly brings salvation to ourselves, but, as a concept, it also presents human life in a strong, positive way. Enlightenment answers the question, "How can human beings find purpose and meaning in life in this transient physical world?" Enlightenment offers a way to heighten our awareness, to understand the purpose and mission of our own lives, and to know the secrets of the universe. Enlightenment is "understanding" in the truest sense, and this understanding gives us great happiness and strength. Enlightenment is not merely about individual development; rather, it signifies the importance of shining our unique individual light.

Prerequisites for Enlightenment

What are the prerequisites for attaining enlightenment? How can we prepare ourselves to become enlightened? There are three preconditions for enlightenment.

First, we need to recognize that human beings have infinite potential. Without this potential, enlightenment would lose all meaning. Enlightenment is impossible if we see human life as a weak, miserable existence that is tossed about in the river of destiny. The fundamental view of Buddhism is that human beings possess infinite goodness within them.

The second prerequisite is aspiration for enlightenment. Aspiration is your heart's desire. The desire to improve ourselves is not something we can receive from someone else. This strong desire for enlightenment needs to spring from within. Awakening to an aspiration for enlightenment is the key, because this aspiration is both our duty and right and is an absolutely necessary condition for attaining enlightenment.

Third, it is necessary to understand and acknowledge

the fact that human beings can achieve results through their own efforts. This is the law of cause and effect that I explained in the previous chapter. To attain enlightenment, you need to accept and understand that you reap what you sow and that your efforts will always bring rewards in the end.

In this world, your efforts may not always be rewarded in tangible forms. In the world of the mind, however, if you sow a seed, it will bear fruit without fail. For example, even if you do something good for others out of good intentions, you might be misunderstood. But in the spirit world, if you hold a kind thought and express it in an action, the result manifests itself instantaneously. In the spirit world, the seeds of your thoughts and actions bear fruit immediately, and you know the results the moment you create the cause.

To conclude this section, let me summarize the three prerequisites for attaining enlightenment: The first is to believe in the infinite potential of human beings. The second is to cultivate an aspiration for enlightenment and have the courage to step forward. The third is to completely believe in the law of cause and effect; know that the seeds you sow and cultivate will bear fruit without fail in the world of enlightenment.

Three Ways of Attaining Enlightenment

What kind of methods should we use to attain enlightenment? Are there any specific ways of working toward this goal? To answer these questions, I would like to suggest the following three ways to attain enlightenment.

The first way is to devote all your time to self-discipline toward the goal of acquiring spiritual wisdom and increasing your level of awareness. In some cases, you may open the window of your mind and experience spiritual phenomena. This is a path that devoted seekers and professional religious practitioners should take. When you follow this path, you devote all your time to the study of the Truths, practice what you learn in your everyday life, and observe the world and yourself from the higher awareness you gain through various experiences of being in contact with the spiritual world. This method has been and still is the main path to enlightenment.

One of the distinctive characteristics of Shakyamuni's order was that it produced "professional" religious practitioners, or those who were expert in religious practices. Perhaps because society was not as complex as it is today, many people in his time did not hesitate to abandon their secular lives to pursue enlightenment. Abandoning secular life meant that they were determined to devote their lives to seeking enlightenment and to becoming "professional" religious practitioners.

Whether it is necessary to abandon secular life to attain enlightenment may be subject to debate. But if you wish to become an expert in any walk of life and accomplish something in this world, you must devote yourself wholeheartedly to reaching your goal. For instance, if you want to be a successful actor, you need to devote yourself to developing your acting skills. To paint a picture that touches people's hearts, artists need to paint hundreds of paintings. Those who paint only as a hobby in their free time will probably never become professional artists. Because Shakyamuni knew this truth, he decided to educate and train his disciples so that they could become expert religious practitioners.

The second way to enlightenment is a path for lay seekers. While making a living in this secular world, you can set your mind free by learning the teachings of the Truths. You can devote all your spare time to exploring, studying, and spreading the Truths. I think that this second path to enlightenment is necessary for the Truths to be disseminated widely. Most people cannot devote all their efforts to the path of Truth and become full-time seekers, so the discipline for lay seekers is very important for many people.

The discipline for lay seekers is different from the discipline for those who enter the priesthood. Training for lay seekers may be more difficult, in a sense, because in their daily lives, lay seekers have to take part in activities that are far from the world of Truth. Lay seekers are disadvantaged in the sense that they cannot fully devote themselves to spiritual discipline; the difficulty of their discipline can be compared to that of running on the sand with weights in one's shoes. But at the same time, constantly seeking the Truths and walking on the path to enlightenment in the midst of adverse circumstances can be excellent training that strengthens the soul. In this sense, lay seekers are in an advantageous position.

The third way to attain enlightenment is to introduce and share your enlightenment in different ways so that it will permeate many different fields in the world. In contrast to the second way to enlightenment, which draws a clear line between secular undertakings and the discipline of the path to Truth, this third way emancipates enlightenment from the religious world and spreads it in the secular world. This requires you to not only seek enlightenment but also share it with others by transforming it into different forms. It is to apply your understanding of the teachings of the Truths to solve issues people face in a wide range of fields, such as art, literature, philosophy, business, and family life.

This third way is not exactly the direct path to enlightenment, but it is a method of enlightenment for those who want to put their learning into practice within the limits of their ability. This is not the way for "professional" seekers, but is a practical and diversified application of self-discipline for lay seekers. This method is centered on the practice of the Truths in daily life, through which the practitioner gains experiences that lead to higher awareness.

The Mechanism of Enlightenment

Next, I would like to explore the mechanism of enlightenment. But before going into the discussion, I would like to talk about the workings of the soul and the mind. Let me begin by defining the soul and the mind.

First of all, the soul is a spiritual energy that resides within the physical body. With my spiritual sight, I can see that the soul takes exactly the same shape as the body—it is of exactly the same size and has eyes, a nose, a mouth, and other features. A soul is originally formless energy, but it takes a life-sized form when it dwells within the physical body.

The mind is the central core of the soul. The mind can be likened to the yolk of an egg. It is the control center of the soul, and visually, it is situated close to the physical heart. The soul is connected to the infinite world through its core, the mind. With spiritual sight, you can see that individual souls exist separately but that the mind acts like a rope or tube that gets connected to the infinite world. This tube acts as a path that leads to many different realms in the spirit world. While human souls coexist with the physical body in the three-dimensional, material world, the mind is connected to the different levels of the spirit world, ranging from the fourth to the ninth dimensions.

This must sound quite mystical, but it is the structure of the world of the mind. The philosophical concept "One is many, and many are one" also describes the world of the mind. Things exist and at the same time do not exist; they don't exist, and at the same time exist. The world of the mind is where things that seem to contradict one another can exist compatibly.

If you could look through the window of your mind, you would see the spirit world right in front of you. It is like looking at the entire city through a telescope in an observatory on top of a high-rise building. If you bring it into focus, you can get a close-up view of busy city streets. You can see mountains in the distance as well. You focus the lens of your mind in the same way to see many different worlds. In fact, enlightenment is a method of controlling the focus of your mind.

The mechanism of enlightenment is related to the existence of different dimensions in the multilayered structure of the spirit world. You can determine the level of your enlightenment by observing how you are able to adjust the direction, degree of magnification, and focal length of the telescope of your mind. You are capable of seeing the world close to you or looking into the distance. The choice is entirely up to you. The many different realms of the spirit world are not far away from where you are. You can feel and live in these worlds at this very moment.

The Three Benefits of Enlightenment

In the previous section, I described the mechanism of attaining enlightenment using the metaphor of controlling the focus of your mind's telescope. What are the benefits of enlightenment? How does enlightenment change our life? What merits does enlightenment bring? These may be the questions you have in your mind now. So, in this section, I would like to discuss the three main benefits of enlightenment.

The first benefit is that, when you attain higher awareness, you will be able to solve worldly issues and problems, eliminating your worries, suffering, and anxieties.

The second benefit of attaining enlightenment is that you can contribute to the happiness of a greater number of people. The more you know about yourself and the world, the more you can help people become truly happy and live a wonderful life. By attaining enlightenment, you can refine your character and have a more beneficent influence on the happiness of people around you.

The third benefit of enlightenment is the feeling of true happiness that it brings. This indescribable feeling of bliss far surpasses the joy that you experience from the things of this world, such as salary raises, promotions, and compliments. Awakening to the Truths is the greatest pleasure a human soul can experience. We need to experience this supreme bliss to live a true life as a human being. Enlightenment is the greatest gift that Eternal Buddha (God) has granted to us human beings through the course of our lives. To become truly human, it is essential that we know this happiness.

To conclude, I would like to summarize the three main benefits of enlightenment:

1. You can eliminate your sufferings with a higher level of awareness.
2. You can benefit a greater number of people.
3. You can savor the supreme bliss that accompanies enlightenment itself.

6 What Is the Arhat State?

The educational objective that Shakyamuni emphasized the most was the attainment of the arhat state. He emphasized the arhat state because it is the first stage of human perfection and because this state of mind allows people to receive communication from divine spirits in heaven. In other words, the arhat state is the first stage in which you experience the existence of the spirit world and live in the way that you would in the spirit world while still living in this world.

The arhat state is equivalent to an enlightenment of the upper level of the World of Light in the sixth dimension. You can attain the enlightenment of the sixth dimension by making the intellectual endeavor to acquire the Truths. The upper level of the sixth dimension is a place where arhats prepare themselves to proceed to the next level, the World of Bodhisattvas in the seventh dimension. The arhat state is the gateway to the World of Bodhisattvas.

Strictly speaking, the arhat state can be broken down into several stages, but here I would like to roughly divide it into two levels. The first stage is called arhat-in-progress, which is a state in which you are still on your way to attaining the arhat state. The second stage is called the fruit-of-arhat, in which you have already reached the arhat state.

What is the difference between the arhat-in-progress state and the fruit-of-arhat state? When you attain the state of arhat-in-progress, you recognize yourself as a devoted practitioner of spiritual disciplines, you can liberate yourself from worries and sufferings, and you are constantly making a diligent effort to advance on the path of Truth. To attain the state of a fruit-of-arhat, you need to maintain the arhat-in-progress state for at least two or three years. You can reach the fruit-of-arhat stage if you can maintain a calm state of mind that is free from any disturbances and worldly attachments for three years. During this period, you also need to practice self-reflection regularly, continue in your discipline on the path of Truth, and receive guidance from heaven. It is necessary to sustain this state of mind for a certain period of time to attain the fruit-of-arhat state.

It is possible for some people to attain the state of arhat-in-progress in a matter of days or a week. They can do this by recalling all their memories since childhood, reflecting on their wrong thoughts and deeds one by one, and allowing tears of repentance ("the rain of Dharma") to cleanse their souls. When they hear the voices of their own guardian spirits and receive light from them as they engage in these practices, they have reached the arhat state.

Although some may reach the arhat-in-progress state very quickly, the key is to sustain this condition. Spending one week on reflective meditation in a remote mountain retreat may allow you to reach a clean state close to the arhat state. However, as soon as you return to ordinary life, your mind gets clouded again. You can attain the state of fruit-of-arhat only if you maintain the clean state of mind for two to three years after you shed tears of repentance and pledge a new beginning. If you leave this world in this state of mind, you will certainly return to the world of the arhat in the upper level of the World of Light in the sixth dimension.

Unfortunately, many of those who have reached the arhat-in-progress state fall back. The way they fall resembles climbers losing ground and tumbling down a mountainside right before they reach the summit. It is possible for virtually anyone to reach the arhat-in-progress state; out of one hundred people, one hundred people can reach this state if they diligently study the teachings of the Truths and continue their self-discipline. But only four or five out of one hundred will be able to achieve the fruit-of-arhat state.

Furthermore, of those who attain the fruit-of-arhat state, less than 10 percent, or ten out of one hundred arhats at most, will be able to enter the World of Bodhisattvas. I have said previously that it is necessary to sustain the arhat state for three years to reach the fruit-of-arhat state. But if you wish to become a bodhisattva, you have to maintain the arhat state throughout a lifetime. A prerequisite to becoming a bodhisattva is to make it a principle to live in the service of others, and this is tantamount to sustaining the state of fruit-of-arhat for a lifetime. As you can see, attaining the state of a bodhisattva is extremely difficult: out of a thousand people who devote themselves to spiritual discipline, only a few will attain the enlightenment of a bodhisattva.

The Discipline of Arhats

In this section, I would like to talk about the discipline of arhats. Out of one thousand seekers, one thousand will be able to reach the arhat-in-progress state if they devote themselves to spiritual discipline under the guidance of good teachers. They can probably manage to sustain this state of mind for a week or two. However, only about fifty of them will be able to attain the fruit-of-arhat state. Furthermore, only about five out of those fifty will become bodhisattvas. This is the difficult challenge that awaits seekers of Truth.

What is the most important way for arhats to progress in their discipline? There are two attitudes an arhat needs to maintain. The first is the willingness to continue in the discipline of refining your mind throughout your lifetime, until the last moment of your life. The human mind gets clouded easily, just as the surface of a mirror gets dirty, so it is necessary to keep polishing your mind every day, in the same manner as you would polish a mirror. This should be part of your daily life. Just as you do the dishes, wash your clothes, and clean your house, you need to refine your mind every day and continue this practice throughout your life.

The second important attitude is humility. The biggest trap for an arhat is conceit. Seekers who have reached the arhat state tend to be easily satisfied with small discoveries of enlightenment and become proud of small successes. When seekers reach the arhat state, they may become able to see others' auras or hear the voices of their own guardian spirits. This often makes seekers mistakenly believe that they are great bodhisattvas of light.

Once you reach the arhat state, it is extremely important that you humbly reflect on yourself. Even if you experience spiritual phenomena, do not be too proud of the fact. Accept it calmly, and have the wisdom to choose what is truly precious. It is vital to maintain the stability of your spiritual senses. There should be no problem if you can take complete control of the spiritual phenomena happening around you, like an expert driver who can maneuver a car at will. But in reality, most people are not capable of this.

So the two most important attitudes to remember as you undergo discipline as an arhat are humility and the diligence to continue refining your mind throughout your life. It is especially important to keep in mind that people can easily get conceited when they experience spiritual phenomena, and we need to remain cautious about falling down from the state of arhat.

The Essential Nature of Bodhisattvas

Following our discussion of the arhat state, let us proceed to the next level, which is the state of bodhisattvas. According to the basic rules of the spirit world, advancing to the World of Bodhisattvas requires one to be born into this world three times while maintaining the state of arhat.

Although human beings repeat cycles of reincarnation numerous times, in almost all cases, the only time they can reach the arhat state is when they learn under a great teacher who has incarnated into this world. It is difficult to reach the arhat state on your own while leading an ordinary life and without a great teacher to learn from. There are some who reach the arhat state through the lessons they learn from the experiences they go through in this world, but these people constitute a very small percentage of arhats.

The majority of people become arhats when they learn from a great spiritual teacher. That's why, when a great teacher is expected to descend to Earth, many spirits wish to be born in the same era. If they study the

Laws of Truth under the guidance of the great teacher and successfully attain the state of arhat, what they learn will remain with them. This ability is like the skills that baseball prayers acquire: once a batter establishes a certain batting average, he will not easily lose the skills that he has built. So once you have attained the enlightenment of an arhat under a great teacher, you need to maintain that state of mind for your next two lives to proceed to reach the state of bodhisattva. It takes three lives in a row, on average, for an arhat to become a bodhisattva.

It is extremely difficult to qualify as a bodhisattva. You have to make constant achievements over a long period of time. The average person reincarnates once every three hundred years, so it takes almost a thousand years, on average, for an arhat to become a bodhisattva. This is how much spiritual discipline is required to become a bodhisattva. If you aim to become a bodhisattva, you need to have the guts to continue making an effort to advance on the path for a thousand years. Unfortunately, most people give up within a few years. It takes exceptionally strong will power, humility, and perseverance to continue spiritual practice for one thousand years. But because it takes enormous effort, the state of bodhisattva that you attain will not be swayed easily.

Bodhisattvas are professional leaders and teachers. The gap between the professional and the amateur is not easy to bridge. You will not be able to become a professional unless you refine yourself intensively and thoroughly. We need to keep in mind that we can't attain the state of bodhisattva instantly; it takes strict self-discipline over a long period of time. It is a mistake to think that we can become a bodhisattva simply by being kind to somebody or making a donation to a charity. It takes tremendous perseverance to continue making tireless efforts on the path to improvement.

Altruism and the spirit of love are the essential nature of bodhisattvas. And behind their love is a unique strength built by their indomitable resolve to make this world a better place to live and their tireless efforts to achieve this goal. This is the spirit of dogged perseverance. Those who are fulfilling their mission as bodhisattvas are those who have kept walking on the narrow and winding path for a long period of time toward the goals of saving others, brightening the world, and creating an ideal world on Earth.

The light that bodhisattvas shine is not superficial glitter. It is an authentic light that shines from deep within their souls as the fruit of their tireless discipline over hundreds and thousands of years.

The Essential Nature of Tathagatas

In the previous section, I said that barely five out of one thousand arhats-in-progress will manage to attain the enlightenment of bodhisattvas and that it will take them a thousand years of self-discipline to do so. So how can bodhisattvas move up to the next stage and become tathagatas? They have to be reincarnated into different regions and eras twenty to thirty times while maintaining the bodhisattva state. In addition, they need to fulfill 80 to 90 percent of their mission each time, regardless of the region and time they were born into. Stability of the soul and outstanding achievements will be required for bodhisattvas to become tathagatas. This means that it takes more than ten thousand years of continued success while maintaining the state of the upper-level bodhisattva. This is an incredibly high hurdle.

Even the bodhisattvas who have made progress and reached the higher state within the World of Bodhisattvas may experience ups and downs and make mistakes over the course of ten thousand years of reincarnations.

They are expected to devote themselves to being of service to and guiding people, but they may, in one of their reincarnations, found a new religion and be misled by evil forces to believe that they are the fundamental God of the universe and to misguide the followers. Even if they make these kinds of mistakes, since they originally possessed a high level of awareness, they will eventually straighten themselves out and come back onto the right path. But in cases like this, they have to start the discipline to become a tathagata all over again. Even if they successfully continue their spiritual discipline as bodhisattvas for several thousand years, if they go astray and spend two or three hundred years rehabilitating their souls, they have to start their discipline all over again.

Continual success over ten thousand years as an upper-level bodhisattva is the prerequisite for becoming a tathagata. Nine thousand years of progress will be nullified if a bodhisattva falls during the remaining one thousand years, and the bodhisattva would then have to start his or her spiritual practice from scratch. Because this discipline is so demanding, only one out of five hundred upper-level bodhisattvas successfully reach the state of a tathagata after ten thousand years of devoted, strenuous discipline.

Based on my observations, there are about two thousand upper-level bodhisattvas who are undergoing discipline to become tathagatas. If we apply the ratio of

500:1, only four out of these two thousand bodhisattvas will successfully attain the state of tathagata. Only four tathagatas are born every ten thousand years, so on average, we see a new tathagata every 2,500 years. There are more than six billion people on Earth and fifty billion including the population of the spirit world. The diligent discipline of all fifty billion people produces only one tathagata every 2,500 years. The path to becoming a tathagata is extremely difficult.

Nevertheless, a birth of new tathagata that happens only once every 2,500 years brings the greatest joy to all humankind. When a new tathagata is born, it lights up the spirit world as brilliantly as if a sparkling chandelier has been lit on the ceiling of heaven. It fills the heavenly spirits with joy and increases the power of heaven.

Spirits in heaven continue to make these strenuous and tireless efforts. A new tathagata becomes a source of spiritual energy that nourishes numerous people, acting like a queen bee that lays innumerable eggs. This energy marks the birth of a new leader whose unshakeable state and superior abilities, developed over ten thousand years of hard work, can guide many people.

I estimate the total number of tathagatas in heaven to be less than five hundred. Considering the fact that they are guiding nearly fifty billion spirits in total, each tathagata is capable of leading as many as one hundred million people. Ten thousand years of successful discipline is required for an upper-level bodhisattva to become a tathagata because they need to develop outstanding leadership abilities to guide such large numbers of people. This may sound like an impossible feat, but this path is open to everyone; everyone has the possibility of becoming a tathagata, as long as they strive to make this outstanding achievement.

The Path to Becoming a Buddha

As I said in the previous section, even an ordinary soul can become a tathagata if it continues tireless efforts of self-discipline. In fact, quite a number of souls that were created on Planet Earth have successfully evolved to become tathagatas.

Above the state of tathagatas is the state of Buddhas. "Buddha" means "awakened one" or "enlightened one," and these souls shine as the saviors of each planet. In the Earth's spirit group, there are ten Buddhas. Buddhas have an incomparable ability to take charge of a planet's entire spirit group. Can you imagine how much effort it requires for a tathagata to become a Buddha or a Grand Tathagata of the ninth dimension? It requires continual successful achievements over at least one hundred million years. Tathagatas can enter the world of saviors, the world of Grand Tathagatas, in the ninth dimension only when they have been successfully guiding humankind for more than one hundred million years through all their reincarnations as tathagatas. While it takes ten thousand years of discipline for an upper-level bodhisattva to become a tathagata, it can take as long as one hundred million years for a tathagata to become a Grand Tathagata.

The five hundred tathagatas in the eighth dimension will have to go through one hundred million years of discipline to evolve into Grand Tathagatas. And even a single failure during this period will bring all their previous efforts to naught, and they will have to start the whole process again from scratch.

In theory, one Grand Tathagata is born every one or two hundred million years. In the Earth's spirit group, however, there has not been a soul created on Earth that has evolved into a Grand Tathagata; all the ten Grand Tathagatas originally came from other planets to create Earth's spirit group. In the upper part of the eighth dimension, called the Sun Realm, there are several divine spirits who have the potential to evolve into Grand Tathagatas. Perhaps a new Grand Tathagata will be born in the next few tens of millions of years.

A new Grand Tathagata may join the other spirits of the ninth dimension, increasing the total number of Great Guiding Spirits, or may replace one of the spirits, who will move to another planet to guide its inhabitants.

As we have seen, human souls are in a process of eternal evolution through endless effort. What it takes to win the ultimate victory of the soul is perseverance and the willingness to work tirelessly. This spirit is celebrated, because it will bring happiness to a great number of people. We must know that bringing happiness to many is the source of our greatest happiness.

Afterword to the Original Edition

You may have let out a sigh on reading the last chapter of this book as you realized how difficult it would be to attain enlightenment. The path to enlightenment is indeed difficult and demanding, but your strong determination will take you to the starting line and serve as the driving force to reach the ultimate goal.

It would be my greatest pleasure, as the author of this book, if this book serves as a guide for your eternal spiritual evolution.

Ryuho Okawa
Master and CEO of Happy Science Group
August 1988

Afterword to the Current Edition

In this revised edition of the original book published in 1988, I have taken a more rigorous approach to Buddhist thought and added discussions of the significance of wisdom and the important role of spiritual powers in attaining enlightenment.

I hope that you will gain a deeper understanding of the essence of Buddhism by reading this book, along with my other publications, *The Challenge of Enlightenment* and *The Rebirth of Buddha.*

Ryuho Okawa
Master and CEO of Happy Science Group
October 1997

About the Author

Founder and CEO of Happy Science Group.

Ryuho Okawa was born on July 7th 1956, in Tokushima, Japan. After graduating from the University of Tokyo with a law degree, he joined a Tokyo-based trading house. While working at its New York headquarters, he studied international finance at the Graduate Center of the City University of New York. In 1981, he attained Great Enlightenment and became aware that he is El Cantare with a mission to bring salvation to all humankind.

In 1986, he established Happy Science. It now has members in 168 countries across the world, with more than 700 branches and temples as well as 10,000 missionary houses around the world.

He has given over 3,500 lectures (of which more than 150 are in English) and published over 3,100 books (of which more than 600 are Spiritual Interview Series), and many are translated into 41 languages. Along with *The Laws of the Sun* and *The Laws of Hell*, many of the books have become best sellers or million sellers. To date, Happy Science has produced 27 movies under the supervision of Okawa. He has given the original story and concept and is also the Executive Producer. He has also composed music and written lyrics of over 450 pieces.

Moreover, he is the Founder of Happy Science University and Happy Science Academy (Junior and Senior High School), Founder and President of the Happiness Realization Party, Founder and Honorary Headmaster of Happy Science Institute of Government and Management, Founder of IRH Press Co., Ltd., and the Chairperson of NEW STAR PRODUCTION Co., Ltd. and ARI Production Co., Ltd.

About Happy Science

Happy Science is a religious group founded on the faith in El Cantare who is the God of the Earth, and the Creator of the universe. The essence of human beings is the soul that was created by God, and we all are children of God. God is our true parent, so in our souls we have a fundamental desire to "believe in God, love God, and get closer to God." And, we can get closer to God by living with God's Will as our own. In Happy Science, we call this the "Exploration of Right Mind." More specifically, it means to practice the Fourfold Path, which consists of "Love, Wisdom, Self-Reflection, and Progress."

Love: Love means "love that gives," or mercy. God hopes for the happiness of all people. Therefore, living with God's Will as our own means to start by practicing "love that gives."

Wisdom: By studying and putting spiritual knowledge into practice, you can cultivate wisdom and become better at resolving problems in life.

Self-Reflection: Once you learn the heart of God and the difference between His mind and yours, you should strive to bring your own mind closer to the mind of God—that process is called self-reflection. Self-reflection also includes meditation and prayer.

Progress: Since God hopes for the happiness of all people, you should also make progress in your love, and make an effort to realize utopia in which everyone in your society, country, and eventually all humankind can become happy.

As we practice this Fourfold Path, our souls will advance toward God step by step. That is when we can attain real happiness—our souls' desire to get closer to God comes true.

In Happy Science, we conduct activities to make ourselves happy through belief in Lord El Cantare, and to spread this faith to the world and bring happiness to all. We welcome you to join our activities!

We hold events and activities to help you practice the Fourfold Path at our branches, temples, missionary centers and missionary houses

Love: We hold various volunteering activities. Our members conduct missionary work together as the greatest practice of love.

Wisdom: We offer our comprehensive books collection, many of which are available online and at Happy Science locations. In addition, we give out numerous opportunities such as seminars or book clubs to learn the Truth.

Self-Reflection: We offer opportunities to polish your mind through self-reflection, meditation, and prayer. There are many cases in which members have experienced improvement in their human relationships by changing their own minds.

Progress: We also offer seminars to enhance your power of influence. Because it is also important to do well at work to make society better, we hold seminars to improve your work and management skills.

Contact Information

Happy Science is a worldwide organization with branches and temples around the globe. For a comprehensive list, visit the worldwide directory at *happy-science.org*. The following are some of our main Happy Science locations:

UNITED STATES AND CANADA

New York
79 Franklin St., New York, NY 10013, USA
Phone: 1-212-343-7972
Fax: 1-212-343-7973
Email: ny@happy-science.org
Website: happyscience-usa.org

New Jersey
66 Hudson St., #2R, Hoboken, NJ 07030, USA
Phone: 1-201-313-0127
Email: nj@happy-science.org
Website: happyscience-usa.org

Chicago
2300 Barrington Rd., Suite #400,
Hoffman Estates, IL 60169, USA
Phone: 1-630-937-3077
Email: chicago@happy-science.org
Website: happyscience-usa.org

Florida
5208 8th St., Zephyrhills, FL 33542, USA
Phone: 1-813-715-0000
Fax: 1-813-715-0010
Email: florida@happy-science.org
Website: happyscience-usa.org

Atlanta
1874 Piedmont Ave., NE Suite 360-C
Atlanta, GA 30324, USA
Phone: 1-404-892-7770
Email: atlanta@happy-science.org
Website: happyscience-usa.org

San Francisco
525 Clinton St.
Redwood City, CA 94062, USA
Phone & Fax: 1-650-363-2777
Email: sf@happy-science.org
Website: happyscience-usa.org

Los Angeles
1590 E. Del Mar Blvd., Pasadena,
CA 91106, USA
Phone: 1-626-395-7775
Fax: 1-626-395-7776
Email: la@happy-science.org
Website: happyscience-usa.org

Orange County
16541 Gothard St. Suite 104
Huntington Beach, CA 92647
Phone: 1-714-659-1501
Email: oc@happy-science.org
Website: happyscience-usa.org

San Diego
7841 Balboa Ave. Suite #202
San Diego, CA 92111, USA
Phone: 1-626-395-7775
Fax: 1-626-395-7776
E-mail: sandiego@happy-science.org
Website: happyscience-usa.org

Hawaii
Phone: 1-808-591-9772
Fax: 1-808-591-9776
Email: hi@happy-science.org
Website: happyscience-usa.org

Kauai
3343 Kanakolu Street, Suite 5
Lihue, HI 96766, USA
Phone: 1-808-822-7007
Fax: 1-808-822-6007
Email: kauai-hi@happy-science.org
Website: happyscience-usa.org

Toronto
845 The Queensway
Etobicoke, ON M8Z 1N6, Canada
Phone: 1-416-901-3747
Email: toronto@happy-science.org
Website: happy-science.ca

Vancouver
#201-2607 East 49th Avenue,
Vancouver, BC, V5S 1J9, Canada
Phone: 1-604-437-7735
Fax: 1-604-437-7764
Email: vancouver@happy-science.org
Website: happy-science.ca

INTERNATIONAL

Tokyo
1-6-7 Togoshi, Shinagawa,
Tokyo, 142-0041, Japan
Phone: 81-3-6384-5770
Fax: 81-3-6384-5776
Email: tokyo@happy-science.org
Website: happy-science.org

London
3 Margaret St.
London, W1W 8RE United Kingdom
Phone: 44-20-7323-9255
Fax: 44-20-7323-9344
Email: eu@happy-science.org
Website: www.happyscience-uk.org

Sydney
516 Pacific Highway, Lane Cove North,
2066 NSW, Australia
Phone: 61-2-9411-2877
Fax: 61-2-9411-2822
Email: sydney@happy-science.org

Sao Paulo
Rua. Domingos de Morais 1154,
Vila Mariana, Sao Paulo SP
CEP 04010-100, Brazil
Phone: 55-11-5088-3800
Email: sp@happy-science.org
Website: happyscience.com.br

Jundiai
Rua Congo, 447, Jd. Bonfiglioli
Jundiai-CEP, 13207-340, Brazil
Phone: 55-11-4587-5952
Email: jundiai@happy-science.org

Seoul
74, Sadang-ro 27-gil,
Dongjak-gu, Seoul, Korea
Phone: 82-2-3478-8777
Fax: 82-2-3478-9777
Email: korea@happy-science.org

Taipei
No. 89, Lane 155, Dunhua N. Road,
Songshan District, Taipei City 105, Taiwan
Phone: 886-2-2719-9377
Fax: 886-2-2719-5570
Email: taiwan@happy-science.org

Taichung
No. 146, Minzu Rd., Central Dist.,
Taichung City 400001, Taiwan (R.O.C.)
Phone: 886-4-22233777
Email: taichung@happy-science.org

Kuala Lumpur
No 22A, Block 2, Jalil Link Jalan Jalil Jaya
2, Bukit Jalil 57000,
Kuala Lumpur, Malaysia
Phone: 60-3-8998-7877
Fax: 60-3-8998-7977
Email: malaysia@happy-science.org
Website: happyscience.org.my

Kathmandu
Kathmandu Metropolitan City,
Ward No. 15, Ring Road, Kimdol,
Sitapaila Kathmandu, Nepal
Phone: 977-1-537-2931
Email: nepal@happy-science.org

Kampala
Plot 877 Rubaga Road, Kampala
P.O. Box 34130 Kampala, UGANDA
Email: uganda@happy-science.org

ABOUT IRH PRESS USA

IRH Press USA Inc. was founded in 2013 as an affiliated firm of IRH Press Co., Ltd. Based in New York, the press publishes books in various categories including spirituality, religion, and self-improvement and publishes books by Ryuho Okawa, the author of over 100 million books sold worldwide. For more information, visit okawabooks.com.

Follow us on:

- Facebook: Okawa Books
- Youtube: Okawa Books
- Pinterest: Okawa Books
- Instagram: OkawaBooks
- Twitter: Okawa Books
- Goodreads: Ryuho Okawa

NEWSLETTER

To receive book related news, promotions and events, please subscribe to our newsletter below.

irhpress.com/pages/subscribe

AUDIO / VISUAL MEDIA

YOUTUBE

PODCAST

Introduction of Ryuho Okawa's titles; topics ranging from self-help, current affairs, spirituality, religion, and the universe.

HIGHLIGHTED TITLE

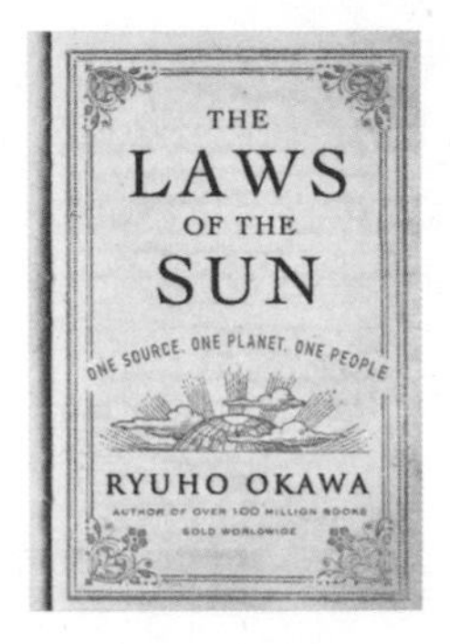

The Laws of the Sun

One Source, One Planet, One People

Paperback • 288 pages • $15.95
ISBN: 978-1-942125-43-3 (Apr. 20, 2021)

Imagine if you could ask God why he created this world and what spiritual laws he used to shape us—and everything around us. Ryuho Okawa outlines these laws of the universe and provides a road map for living one's life with greater purpose and meaning. This powerful book shows the way to realize true happiness—a happiness that continues from this world through the other.

The Laws of Hell

"IT" follows.....

Paperback • 264 pages • $17.95
ISBN: 978-1-958655-04-7 (May 1, 2023)

Whether you believe it or not, the Spirit World and hell do exist, and unfortunately, 1 in 2 people are falling to hell. To stop hell from spreading and to save the souls of all human beings, the Spiritual Master, Ryuho Okawa has compiled vital teachings in this book. This publication marks his 3,100th book and is the one and only comprehensive Truth about the modern hell.

BUDDHIST TITLES

The Challenge of Enlightenment

Now, Here, the New Dharma Wheel Turns

Paperback • 380 pages • $17.95
ISBN: 978-1-942125-92-1 (Dec. 20, 2022)

Buddha's teachings, a reflection of his eternal wisdom, are like a bamboo pole used to change the course of your boat in the rapid stream of the great river called life. By reading this book, your mind becomes clearer, learns to savor inner peace, and it will empower you to make profound life improvements.

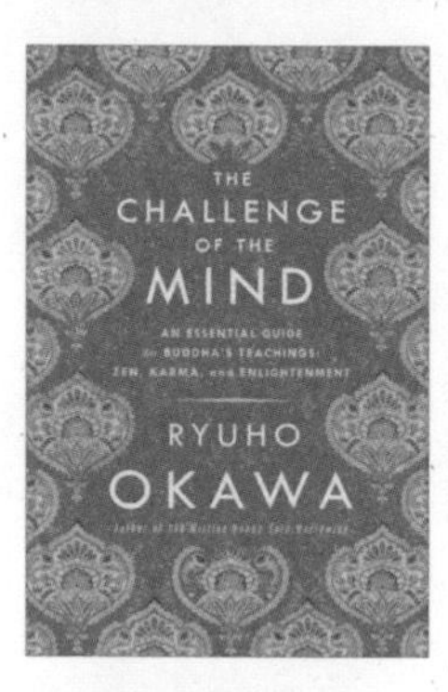

The Challenge of the Mind

An Essential Guide to Buddha's Teachings: Zen, Karma and Enlightenment

Paperback • 208 pages • $16.95
ISBN: 978-1-942125-45-7 (Nov. 15, 2018)

In this book, Ryuho Okawa explains essential Buddhist tenets and how to put them into practice. Enlightenment is not just an abstract idea but one that everyone can experience to some extent. Okawa offers a solid basis of reason and intellectual understanding to Buddhist concepts. By applying these basic principles to our lives, we can direct our minds to higher ideals and create a bright future for ourselves and others.

The True Eightfold Path

Guideposts for Self-Innovation

Paperback • 256 pages • $16.95
ISBN: 978-1-942125-80-8 (Mar. 30, 2021)

This book explains how we can apply the Eightfold Path, one of the main pillars of Shakyamuni Buddha's teachings, as everyday guideposts in the modern-age to achieve self-innovation to live better and make positive changes in these uncertain times.

The Laws of Great Enlightenment

Always Walk with Buddha

Paperback • 232 pages • $17.95
ISBN: 978-1-942125-62-4 (Nov. 7, 2019)

Constant self-blame for mistakes, setbacks, or failures and feelings of unforgivingness toward others are hard to overcome. Through the power of enlightenment we can learn to forgive ourselves and others, overcome life's problems, and courageously create a brighter future ourselves. *The Laws of Great Enlightenment* addresses the core problems of life that people often struggle with and offers advice on how to overcome them based on spiritual truths.

Rojin, Buddha's Mystical Power

Its Ultimate Attainment in Today's World

Paperback • 224 pages • $16.95
ISBN: 978-1-942125-82-2 (Sep. 24, 2021)

In this book, Ryuho Okawa has redefined the traditional Buddhist term *Rojin* and explained that in modern society it means the following: the ability for individuals with great spiritual powers to live in the world as people with common sense while using their abilities to the optimal level. This book will unravel the mystery of the mind and lead you to the path to enlightenment.

The Rebirth of Buddha

My Eternal Disciples, Hear My Words

Paperback • 280 pages • $17.95
ISBN: 978-1-942125-95-2 (Jul. 15, 2022)

These are the messages of Buddha who has returned to this modern age as promised to His eternal beloved disciples. They are in simple words and poetic style, yet contain profound messages. Once you start reading these passages, your soul will be replenished as the plant absorbs the water, and you will remember why you chose this era to be born into with Buddha. Listen to the voices of your Eternal Master and awaken to your calling.

Other Books by Ryuho Okawa

Words for Building Character

Words for Life

Words for Work

The Nine Dimensions
Unveiling the Laws of Eternity

The Ten Principles from El Cantare Volume I
Ryuho Okawa's First Lectures on His Basic Teachings

The Ten Principles from El Cantare Volume II
Ryuho Okawa's First Lectures on His Wish to Save the World

Developmental Stages of Love
– The Original Theory
Philosophy of Love in My Youth

The Power of Basics
Introduction to Modern Zen Life of
Calm, Spirituality and Success

The Strong Mind
The Art of Building the Inner Strength to
Overcome Life's Difficulties

The Royal Road of Life
Beginning Your Path of Inner Peace, Virtue, and a Life of Purpose

The Unhappiness Syndrome
28 Habits of Unhappy People (and How to Change Them)

The Miracle of Meditation
Opening Your Life to Peace, Joy, and the Power Within

For a complete list of books, visit *OkawaBooks.com*.